LOC

C000059783

SIX ~~EDITION~~

2019

The complete guide to all
Locomotives which operate on
the national railway
and Eurotunnel networks

Robert Pritchard & Peter Hall

ISBN 978 1909 431 47 8

© 2018. Platform 5 Publishing Ltd, 52 Broadfield Road, Sheffield, S8 0XJ,
England.

Printed in England by The Lavenham Press, Lavenham, Suffolk.

CONTENTS

PROVISION OF INFORMATION

This book has been compiled with care to be as accurate as possible, but some information is not easily available and the publisher cannot be held responsible for any errors or omissions. We would like to thank the companies and individuals who have been helpful in supplying information to us. The authors of this series of books are always pleased to receive notification of any inaccuracies that may be found, to enhance future editions. Please send comments to:

Robert Pritchard, Platform 5 Publishing Ltd, 52 Broadfield Road, Sheffield, S8 0XJ, England.

e-mail: robert.pritchard@platform5.com   **Tel:** 0114 255 2625.

This book is updated to information received by 15 October 2018.

UPDATES

This book is updated to the Stock Changes given in **Today's Railways UK 203** (November 2018). The Platform 5 railway magazine **"Today's Railways UK"** publishes Stock Changes every month to update this book. The magazine also contains news and rolling stock information on the railways of Great Britain and Ireland and is published on the second Monday of every month. For further details of **Today's Railways UK**, please contact Platform 5 Publishing Ltd.

Front cover photograph: Pullman Car Company-liveried 67024 and 67021 are seen at St Austell with the 12.15 Truro–London Victoria on 29/04/18. **Tony Christie**

BRITAIN'S RAILWAY SYSTEM

INFRASTRUCTURE & OPERATION

Britain's national railway infrastructure is owned by a "not for dividend" company, Network Rail. In 2014 Network Rail was reclassified as a public sector company, being described by the Government as a "public sector arm's-length body of the Department for Transport".

Most stations and maintenance depots are leased to and operated by Train Operating Companies (TOCs), but some larger stations are controlled by Network Rail. The only exception is the infrastructure on the Isle of Wight: The Island Line franchise uniquely included maintenance of the infrastructure as well as the operation of passenger services. As Island Line is now part of the South Western Railway franchise, both the infrastructure and trains are operated by South Western Railway.

Trains are operated by TOCs over Network Rail tracks (the National Network), regulated by access agreements between the parties involved. In general, TOCs are responsible for the provision and maintenance of the locomotives, rolling stock and staff necessary for the direct operation of services, whilst Network Rail is responsible for the provision and maintenance of the infrastructure and also for staff to regulate the operation of services.

The Department for Transport (DfT) is the franchising authority for the national network, with Transport Scotland overseeing the award of the ScotRail franchise and the Welsh Government overseeing the Wales & Borders franchise.

A franchise is the right to run specified services within a specified area for a period of time, in return for the right to charge fares and, where appropriate, to receive financial support from the Government. Subsidy is payable in respect of socially necessary services. Service standards are monitored by the DfT throughout the duration of the franchise. Franchisees earn revenue primarily from fares and from subsidy. They generally lease stations from Network Rail and earn rental income by sub-letting parts of them, for example to retailers.

Franchisees' main costs are the track access charges they pay to Network Rail, the costs of leasing stations and rolling stock and of employing staff. Franchisees may do light maintenance work on rolling stock or contract it out to other companies. Heavy maintenance is normally carried out by the Rolling Stock Leasing Companies, according to contracts.

TOCs can take commercial risks, although some franchises are "management contracts", where ticket revenues pass directly to the DfT. Concessions (such as London Overground) see the operator paid a fee to run the service, usually within tightly specified guidelines. Operators running a concession would not normally take commercial risks, although there are usually penalties and rewards in the contract.

Note that a railway "reporting period" is four weeks.

DOMESTIC PASSENGER TRAIN OPERATORS

The majority of passenger trains are operated by Train Operating Companies on fixed-term franchises or concessions. Expiry dates are shown in the list below:

Franchise	Franchisee	Trading Name
Caledonian Sleeper	Serco	**Caledonian Sleeper**
	(until 31 March 2030)	

This franchise started in April 2015 when operation of the ScotRail and ScotRail Sleeper franchises was separated. Abellio won the ScotRail franchise and Serco the Caledonian Sleeper franchise. Caledonian Sleeper operates four trains nightly between London Euston and Scotland using locomotives hired principally from GBRf. New CAF Mark 5 rolling stock will be introduced in spring 2019 to replace the current Mark 2 and Mark 3 carriages that are used.

Chiltern	Arriva (Deutsche Bahn)	**Chiltern Railways**
	(until 31 December 2021)	

There is an option to extend the franchise by 7 months to July 2022.

Chiltern Railways operates a frequent service between London Marylebone, Banbury and Birmingham Snow Hill, with some peak trains extending to Kidderminster. There are also regular services from Marylebone to Stratford-upon-Avon and to Aylesbury Vale Parkway via Amersham (along the London Underground Metropolitan Line). A new route to Oxford Parkway and then Oxford was added in 2015–16. The fleet consists of DMUs of Classes 165, 168 and 172 plus a number of locomotive-hauled rakes used on some of the Birmingham route trains, worked by Class 68s hired from DRS.

Cross Country	Arriva (Deutsche Bahn)	**CrossCountry**
	(until further notice)	

Franchise was due to finish in December 2019 (with an option to extend it to November 2020), but in September 2018 it was announced that the competition for the next franchise had been stopped, pending the publication of a Rail Review by the Government.

CrossCountry operates a network of long distance services between Scotland, the North-East of England and Manchester to the South-West of England, Reading, Southampton, Bournemouth and Guildford, centred on Birmingham New Street. These trains are mainly formed of diesel Class 220/221 Voyagers, supplemented by a small number of HSTs on the NE–SW route. Inter-urban services also link Nottingham, Leicester and Stansted Airport with Birmingham and Cardiff. These trains use Class 170 DMUs.

Crossrail	MTR	**TfL Rail**
	(until 30 May 2023)	

There is an option to extend the concession by 2 years to May 2025.

This is a new concession which started in May 2015. Initially Crossrail took over the Liverpool Street–Shenfield stopping service from Greater Anglia, using a fleet of Class 315 EMUs, with the service branded "TfL Rail". New Class 345 EMUs are now being introduced on this route and are also used between Paddington and Hayes & Harlington (both in 7-car formation). TfL Rail currently also operates the former Heathrow Connect stopping service that uses Class 360 EMUs. From autumn 2019 Crossrail will operate through new tunnels beneath central London, from Shenfield and Abbey Wood in the east to Reading and Heathrow Airport in the west. It will then be branded "Elizabeth Line".

East Coast
London North Eastern Railway

Franchise awarded to Stagecoach/Virgin Trains in 2015 but was terminated just over 3 years later in 2018 (having originally been due to operate until 2023) after the franchise failed. Currently operated on an interim basis by the DfT's "Operator of Last Resort". It is due to be relet in 2020 as part of a new public/private East Coast partnership.

LNER operates frequent long distance trains on the East Coast Main Line between London King's Cross, Leeds, York, Newcastle and Edinburgh, with less frequent services to Bradford, Harrogate, Skipton, Hull, Lincoln, Glasgow, Aberdeen and Inverness. A mixed fleet of Class 91s and 30 Mark 4 sets, and 15 HST sets, are used on these trains. Two Class 90s are hired from DB Cargo as cover for the Class 91 fleet on an as-required basis. A new fleet of Hitachi IEP trains are due to be introduced from late 2018.

East Midlands
Stagecoach Group
(until 17 August 2019)
East Midlands Trains

There is an option to extend the franchise until 17 August 2020.

EMT operates a mix of long distance high speed services on the Midland Main Line (MML), from London St Pancras to Sheffield (to Leeds at peak times and with some extensions to York/Scarborough), Nottingham (plus peak-hour trains to Lincoln) and Corby, and local and regional services ranging from the Norwich–Liverpool route to Nottingham–Skegness, Newark–Mansfield–Worksop, Newark–Matlock and Derby–Crewe. It also operates local services in Lincolnshire. Trains on the MML are worked by a fleet of Class 222 DMUs and nine HSTs, whilst the local and regional fleet consists of DMU Classes 153, 156 and 158.

East Anglia
Abellio (Netherlands Railways)/Mitsui Group
(until 15 October 2025)
Greater Anglia

There is an option to extend the franchise by 1 year to October 2026.

Greater Anglia operates main line trains between London Liverpool Street, Ipswich and Norwich and local trains across Norfolk, Suffolk and parts of Cambridgeshire. It also runs local and commuter services into Liverpool Street from the Great Eastern (including Southend, Braintree and Clacton) and West Anglia (including Ely/Cambridge and Stansted Airport) routes. It operates a varied fleet of Class 90s with locomotive-hauled Mark 3 sets, DMUs of Classes 153, 156 and 170 and EMUs of Classes 317, 321, 360 and 379. One locomotive-hauled Mark 2 set, using Class 37s, is currently hired for use on some trains between Norwich and Great Yarmouth/Lowestoft.

Essex Thameside
Trenitalia
(until 8 November 2029)
c2c

There is an option to extend the franchise by 6 months to May 2030.

c2c operates an intensive, principally commuter, service from London Fenchurch Street to Southend and Shoeburyness via both Upminster and Tilbury. The fleet consists of 74 Class 357 EMUs, plus six Class 387s.

Great Western
First Group
(until 1 April 2020)
Great Western Railway

Direct Award extension expected to April 2022, with the option of a further 2 year extension to April 2024.

Great Western Railway operates long distance trains from London Paddington to South Wales, the West Country and Worcester and Hereford. In addition there are frequent trains along the Thames Valley corridor to Newbury/Bedwyn and Oxford, plus local and regional trains throughout the South-West including the Cornish, Devon and Thames Valley branches, the Reading–Gatwick North Downs Line and Cardiff–Portsmouth Harbour and Bristol–Weymouth regional routes. A fleet of HSTs is used on the long-distance trains, but these are currently being replaced by new Class 800/802 bi-mode InterCity Express Trains. DMUs of Classes 165 and 166 are used on the Thames Valley, Worcester and North Downs routes as well as on local services around Bristol. Class 387 EMUs are used between Paddington, Reading and Didcot Parkway. Classes 143, 150, 153 and 158 are used on local and regional trains in the South-West. A small fleet of Class 57s is maintained to principally work the overnight "Cornish Riviera" Sleeper service between London Paddington and Penzance.

London Rail	Arriva (Deutsche Bahn) (until May 2024)	**London Overground**

This is a concession and is different from other rail franchises, as fares and service levels are set by Transport for London instead of by the DfT. There is an option to extend the concession by 2 years to May 2026.

London Overground operates services on the Richmond–Stratford North London Line and the Willesden Junction–Clapham Junction West London Line, plus the East London Line from Highbury & Islington to New Cross and New Cross Gate, with extensions to Clapham Junction (via Denmark Hill), Crystal Palace and West Croydon. It also runs services from London Euston to Watford Junction. All these use Class 378 EMUs. Class 172 DMUs are used on the Gospel Oak–Barking route, but will be replaced by new Class 710 EMUs in late 2018. London Overground also operates some suburban services from London Liverpool Street – to Chingford, Enfield Town and Cheshunt. These use Class 315 and 317 EMUs, but will be replaced by Class 710s in 2019.

Merseyrail Electrics	Serco/Abellio (Netherlands Railways) (until 19 July 2028)	**Merseyrail**

Under the control of Merseytravel PTE instead of the DfT. Franchise reviewed every five years to fit in with the Merseyside Local Transport Plan.

Merseyrail operates services between Liverpool and Southport, Ormskirk, Kirkby, Hunts Cross, New Brighton, West Kirby, Chester and Ellesmere Port, using Class 507 and 508 EMUs.

Northern	Arriva (Deutsche Bahn) (until 31 March 2025)	**Northern**

There is an option to extend the franchise by 1 year to March 2026.

Northern operates a range of inter-urban, commuter and rural services throughout the North of England, including those around the cities of Leeds, Manchester, Sheffield, Liverpool and Newcastle. The network extends from Chathill in the north to Nottingham in the south, and Cleethorpes in the east to St Bees in the west. Long distance services include Leeds–Carlisle, Middlesbrough–Carlisle and York–Blackpool North. The operator uses a large fleet of DMUs of Classes 142, 144, 150, 153, 155, 156, 158 and 170 plus EMU Classes 319, 321, 322, 323 and 333. Two locomotive-hauled Mark 2 sets, with Class 37s, are hired from DRS for use on some trains between Carlisle and Barrow-in-Furness as part of a 4-year contract that started in May 2015. New DMUs (Class 195) and EMUs (Class 331) will be introduced from late 2018.

ScotRail	Abellio (Netherlands Railways) (until 31 March 2022)	**ScotRail**

There is an option to extend the franchise by 3 years to March 2025.

ScotRail provides almost all passenger services within Scotland and also trains from Glasgow to Carlisle via Dumfries, some of which extend to Newcastle (jointly operated with Northern). The company operates a large fleet of DMUs of Classes 156, 158 and 170 and EMU Classes 314, 318, 320, 334, 365, 380 and 385. Two locomotive-hauled Mark 2 sets are also used on Fife Circle commuter trains, hauled by Class 68s hired from DRS. In autumn 2018 the first of a fleet of refurbished HSTs entered service between Edinburgh and Aberdeen.

| **South Eastern** | Govia (Go-Ahead/Keolis) (until 31 March 2019) | **Southeastern** |

Southeastern operates all services in the South-East London suburbs, the whole of Kent and part of Sussex, which are primarily commuter services to London. It also operates domestic high speed trains on HS1 from London St Pancras to Ashford, Ramsgate, Dover and Faversham with additional peak services on other routes. EMUs of Classes 375, 376, 377, 465 and 466 are used, along with Class 395s on the High Speed trains.

| **South Western** | First Group/MTR (until 18 August 2024) | **South Western Railway** |

There is an option to extend the franchise by 11 months to July 2025.

South Western Railway operates trains from London Waterloo to destinations across the South and South-West including Woking, Basingstoke, Southampton, Portsmouth, Salisbury, Exeter, Reading and Weymouth as well as suburban services from Waterloo. SWR also runs services between Ryde and Shanklin on the Isle of Wight, using former London Underground 1938 stock (Class 483s). The rest of the fleet consists of DMU Classes 158 and 159 and EMU Classes 444, 450, 455, 456, 458 and 707.

| **Thameslink, Southern & Great Northern (TSGN)** | Govia (Go-Ahead/Keolis) (until 19 September 2021) | **Govia Thameslink Railway** |

There is an option to extend the franchise by 2 years to September 2023.

Govia operates this franchise, the largest in Great Britain, as a management contract. The former Southern franchise was combined with Thameslink/Great Northern in 2015. GTR uses four brands within the franchise: "Thameslink" for trains between Cambridge North, Peterborough, Bedford and Rainham, Sevenoaks, East Grinstead, Brighton, Littlehampton and Horsham via central London and also on the Sutton/Wimbledon loop using new Class 700 EMUs. "Great Northern" comprises services from London King's Cross and Moorgate to Welwyn Garden City, Hertford North, Peterborough, Cambridge and King's Lynn using Class 313, 365 and 387 EMUs. The Class 313s will start to be replaced by new Class 717s late in 2018. "Southern" operates predominantly commuter services between London, Surrey and Sussex and "metro" services in South London, as well as services along the South Coast between Southampton, Brighton, Hastings and Ashford, plus the cross-London service from South Croydon to Milton Keynes. Class 171 DMUs are used on Ashford–Eastbourne and London Bridge–Uckfield services, whilst all other services are in the hands of Class 313, 377, 455 and 700 EMUs. Finally, the premium "Gatwick Express" operates non-stop trains between London Victoria, Gatwick Airport and Brighton using Class 387/2 EMUs.

| **Trans-Pennine Express** | First Group (until 31 March 2023) | **TransPennine Express** |

There is an option to extend the franchise by 2 years to March 2025.

TransPennine Express operates predominantly long distance inter-urban services linking major cities across the North of England, along with Edinburgh and Glasgow in Scotland. The main services are Manchester Airport/Manchester Piccadilly–Newcastle/Middlesbrough/Hull plus Liverpool–Scarborough and Liverpool–Newcastle along the North Trans-Pennine route via Huddersfield, Leeds and York, and Manchester Airport–Cleethorpes along the South Trans-Pennine route via Sheffield. TPE also operates Manchester Airport–Edinburgh/Glasgow. The fleet consists of Class 185 DMUs, plus Class 350 EMUs used on Manchester Airport–Scotland services. Three new fleets are due to be introduced in 2018–19, loco-hauled Class 68+CAF Mark 5A sets, Class 397 EMUs and Class 802 bi-modes.

| **Wales & Borders** | KeolisAmey
(until 14 October 2033) | **Transport for Wales** |

New franchise starting as this book closed for press, procured by the Welsh Government.

Transport for Wales Rail operates a mix of long distance, regional and local services throughout Wales, including the Valley Lines network of lines around Cardiff, and also through services to the English border counties and to Manchester and Birmingham. The fleet consists of DMUs of Classes 142, 143, 150, 158 and 175 and two locomotive-hauled Mark 3 sets: one used on a premium Welsh Government sponsored service on the Cardiff–Holyhead route, and one used between Manchester/Crewe and Holyhead (both are hauled by a Class 67).

| **West Coast Partnership** | Virgin Rail Group (Virgin/Stagecoach Group)
(until 31 March 2020) | **Virgin Trains** |

Virgin Trains operates long distance services along the West Coast Main Line from London Euston to Birmingham/Wolverhampton, Manchester, Liverpool, Blackpool North and Glasgow using Class 390 Pendolino EMUs. It also operates Class 221 Voyagers on the Euston–Chester–Holyhead route, whilst a mixture of Class 221s and 390s are used on the Euston–Birmingham–Glasgow/Edinburgh route.

| **West Midlands Trains** | Abellio/JR East/Mitsui
(until March 2026) | **West Midlands Railway/
London Northwestern** |

There is an option to extend the franchise by 2 years to March 2028.

West Midlands Trains operates services under two brand names. West Midlands Railway trains are local and regional services around Birmingham, including to Stratford-upon-Avon, Worcester, Hereford, Redditch, Rugeley and Shrewsbury. WMR is managed by a consortium of 16 councils and the Department for Transport. London Northwestern is the brand used for long distance and regional services from London Euston to Northampton and Birmingham/Crewe and also between Birmingham and Liverpool, Bedford–Bletchley and Watford Junction–St Albans Abbey. The fleet consists of DMU Classes 150, 153, 170 and 172 and EMU Classes 319, 323 and 350.

NON-FRANCHISED SERVICES

The following operators run non-franchised, or "open access" services (* special seasonal services):

| Operator | Trading Name | Route |

Heathrow Airport Holdings Heathrow Express London Paddington–Heathrow Airport
Heathrow Express operates a frequent express passenger service between London Paddington and Heathrow Airport using Class 332 EMUs.

| Hull Trains
(part of First) | Hull Trains | London King's Cross–Hull |

Hull Trains operates seven trains a day (weekdays) from Hull to London King's Cross via the East Coast Main Line using Class 180 DMUs. One train in each direction starts back from and extends to Beverley.

| Grand Central
(part of Arriva) | Grand Central | London King's Cross–Sunderland/
Bradford Interchange |

Grand Central operates five trains a day from Sunderland and four trains a day from Bradford Interchange to London King's Cross using Class 180 DMUs.

| North Yorkshire Moors Railway Enterprises | North Yorkshire Moors Railway | Pickering–Grosmont–Whitby/ Battersby, Sheringham–Cromer* |

The North Yorkshire Moors Railway operates services on the national network between Grosmont and Whitby or Grosmont and Battersby as an extension of its Pickering–Grosmont services and also operates services between Sheringham and Cromer on behalf of the North Norfolk Railway.

| Vintage Trains | Vintage Trains | Birmingham Snow Hill–Stratford-upon-Avon* |

| West Coast Railway Company | West Coast Railway Company | Fort William–Mallaig* York–Settle–Carlisle* |

WCRC operates steam-hauled services on these routes on a seasonal basis.

INTERNATIONAL PASSENGER OPERATORS

Eurostar International operates passenger services between London St Pancras and mainland Europe. The company, established in 2010, is jointly owned by SNCF (the national operator of France): 55%, SNCB (the national operator of Belgium): 5% and Patina Rail: 40%. Patina Rail is made up of Canadian-based Caisse de dépôt et placement du Québec (CDPG) and UK-based Hermes Infrastructure (owning 30% and 10% respectively). This 40% was previously owned by the UK Government until it was sold in 2015.

In addition, a service for the conveyance of accompanied road vehicles through the Channel Tunnel is provided by the tunnel operating company, Eurotunnel. All Eurotunnel services are operated in top-and-tail mode by the powerful Class 9 Bo-Bo-Bo locomotives.

FREIGHT TRAIN OPERATORS

The following operators operate freight services or empty passenger stock workings under "Open Access" arrangements:

Colas Rail: Colas Rail operates a number of On-Track Machines and also supplies infrastructure monitoring trains for Network Rail. It also operates a number of different freight flows, including oil and timber. Colas Rail has a small but varied fleet consisting of Class 37s, 56s, 66s, 67s and 70s.

DB Cargo (UK): Still the biggest freight operator in the country, DBC (EWS until bought by Deutsche Bahn, when it was initially called DB Schenker) provides a large number of infrastructure trains to Network Rail and also operates coal, steel, intermodal and aggregate trains nationwide. The core fleet is Class 66s. Of the original 250 ordered, 79 have moved to DB's French and Polish operations, although some of the French locos do return to the UK when major maintenance is required. Around 15–20 Class 60s are also used on heavier trains, the remainder of the fleet has been stored or sold.

DBC's six Class 59/2s are used alongside the Mendip Rail 59/0s and 59/1s on stone traffic from the Mendip quarries and around the South-East. DBC's fleet of Class 67s are used on passenger or standby duties for Wales & Borders and LNER and also on excursions or special trains. Class 90s see some use on West Coast Main Line freight traffic and two are also hired to LNER on an as-required basis for use on passenger trains. The Class 92s are mainly used on a limited number of overnight freights on High Speed 1.

DBC also operates the Class 325 EMUs for Royal Mail and a number of excursion trains.

Devon & Cornwall Railways (part of Cappagh Construction Contractors (London)): DCRail specialises in short-term freight haulage contracts, mainly using its two Class 56s.

Direct Rail Services: DRS has built on its original nuclear flask traffic to operate a number of different services. The main flows are intermodal plus the provision of crews and locomotives to Network Rail for autumn Railhead Treatment Trains and also infrastructure trains. DRS has a varied fleet of locomotives, with Class 20s, 37s, 57s and 66s working alongside new Class 68s and diesel-electric Class 88s. Class 68s are hired to Chiltern Railways and ScotRail for passenger trains. Its Class 57s and 68s are used on excursion work.

Freightliner: Freightliner (owned by Genesee & Wyoming) operates container trains from the main Ports at Southampton, Felixstowe, Tilbury and Thamesport to major cities including London, Manchester, Leeds and Birmingham. It also operates trains of coal, cement, infrastructure and aggregates. Most services are worked by Class 66s, with Class 70s mainly used on some of the heavier intermodal trains. A small fleet of Class 86 and 90 electrics are used on intermodal trains on the Great Eastern and West Coast Main Lines, the Class 86s mainly being used in pairs on the WCML between Crewe and Coatbridge.

GB Railfreight: GBRf, owned by the Hector Rail group, operates a mixture of traffic types, mainly using Class 66s together with a small fleet of Class 73s on infrastructure duties and test trains in the South-East and ten Class 60s acquired from Colas Rail in 2018. A growing fleet of Class 92s is also used on some intermodal flows to/from Dollands Moor or through the Channel Tunnel to Calais. Traffic includes coal, intermodal, biomass, aggregates and gypsum as well as infrastructure services for Network Rail and London Underground. GBRf also supplies locomotives to Caledonian Sleeper and owns three Class 47s.

GBRf also operates some excursion trains, including those using the preserved Class 201 "Hastings" DEMU.

Loram (UK): Loram has a freight license and operates a limited number of trains, most hauling On-Track Machines using hired-in locomotives.

Rail Operations Group: This company mainly facilitates rolling stock movements by providing drivers or using locomotives hired from other companies or by using its own fleet of Class 47s. ROG also operates a small number of excursion trains.

West Coast Railway Company: WCRC has a freight licence but doesn't operate any freight as such – only empty stock movements. Its fleet of Class 47s, supplemented by a smaller number of Class 33s, 37s and 57s, is used on excursion work nationwide.

In addition, Amey, Balfour Beatty Rail, Harsco Rail, South Western Railway, Swietelsky Babcock Rail (SB Rail) and VolkerRail operate trains formed of On-Track Machines.

INTRODUCTION

This book contains details of all locomotives which can run on Britain's national railway network, plus those of Eurotunnel.

Locomotives currently approved for use on the national railway network fall into the four broad types: passenger, freight, mixed traffic and shunting.

Passenger
The number of dedicated passenger locomotives has not changed significantly in recent years. However, the number is expected to decline in the future as new multiple unit stock replaces some of the remaining locomotive-hauled or propelled trains. Classes 43 (HST) and 91 and some members of Classes 57, 67, 68, 73/9, 90 and 92 are dedicated to franchised and Open Access passenger operations. Excursion trains have a few dedicated locomotives but mainly use locomotives that are best described as mixed traffic.

Freight
By far the most numerous locomotives are those used solely for bulk commodity and intermodal freight. Since 1998 a large number of new Class 66 locomotives have replaced many former BR designs and in more recent years smaller numbers of Class 70s have also been introduced. There are however a significant number of BR era Class 20, 37, 47, 56, 60, 73/1, 86, 90 and 92 locomotives still in use; their number has increased slightly recently as some locomotives have been reinstated to cope with demand. In addition there is a small fleet of Class 59s acquired privately in the 1980s and 1990s and a small number of re-engined Class 57s in use.

Mixed Traffic
In addition to their use on passenger and commodity freight workings these locomotives are used for stock movements and specialist infrastructure and test trains. The majority, but not all, are fitted with Electric Train Supply. Locomotives from Classes 20, 33, 37, 47, 57, 67, 68, 73/9, 88 and 90 fall into this category. Also included under this heading are preserved locomotives permitted to operate on the national railway network. Although these have in the past solely operated excursion trains they are increasingly seeing occasional use on other types of trains.

Shunting
Very few shunting locomotives are now permitted to operate freely on the National Railway network. The small number that are have to be fitted with a plethora of safety equipment in order to have engineering acceptance. They are mainly used for local workings such as trips between yards or stock movements between depots and stations. Otherwise, shunting locomotives are not permitted to venture from depots or yards onto the National Railway network other than into defined limits within interface infrastructure. Generally such locomotives, which include an increasing number of remotely controlled driverless types, are not included in this book. However, all ex-BR shunting locomotives are listed in this book under Section 1.1 "Diesel Shunting Locomotives".

Locomotives which are owned by, for example, DB Cargo or Freightliner, which have been withdrawn from service and are awaiting disposal are listed in the main part of the book. Locomotives which are awaiting disposal at scrapyards are listed in the "Locomotives Awaiting Disposal" section.

Only preserved locomotives which are currently used on the National Railway network are included. Others, which may still be Network Rail registered but not at present certified for use, are not included, but can be found in the Platform 5 book, "Preserved Locomotives of British Railways".

LAYOUT OF INFORMATION

Locomotive classes are listed in numerical order of class. Principal details and dimensions are quoted for each class in metric and/or imperial units as considered appropriate bearing in mind common UK usage.

The heading "Total" indicates how many of that particular class are listed in this book.

Where numbers actually carried are different from those officially allocated, these are noted in class headings where appropriate. Where locomotives have been recently renumbered, the most immediate previous number is shown in parentheses. Each locomotive entry is laid out as in the following example:

No.	Detail	Livery	Owner	Pool		Allocn.	Name
59206	*b	**DB**	DB	WDAM		MD	John F. Yeoman Rail Pioneer

Detail Differences. Only detail differences which currently affect the areas and types of train which locomotives may work are shown. All other detail differences are excluded. Where such differences occur within a class or part class, they are shown in the "Detail" column alongside the individual locomotive number.

Codes: Codes are used to denote the livery, owner, pool and depot of each locomotive. Details of these will be found in section 6 of this book.

The owner is the responsible custodian of the locomotive and this may not always be the legal owner. Actual ownership can be very complicated. Some vehicles are owned by finance/leasing companies. Others are owned by subsidiary companies of a holding company or by an associate company of the responsible custodian or operator.

Depot allocation codes for all locomotives are shown in this book (apart from shunting locomotives (Classes 03, 07, 08 & 09) where the actual location of each is shown). It should be noted that today much locomotive maintenance is undertaken away from these depots. This may be undertaken at fuelling points, berthing sidings or similar, or by mobile maintenance teams. Therefore locomotives in particular may not return to their "home" depots as often as in the past.

(S) denotes that the locomotive is stored (the actual location is shown).

Names: Only names carried with official sanction are listed. Names are shown in UPPER/lower case characters as actually shown on the name carried on the locomotive.

GENERAL INFORMATION

CLASSIFICATION AND NUMBERING

All locomotives are classified and allocated numbers under the TOPS numbering system, introduced in 1972. This comprises a two-digit class number followed by a three-digit serial number.

For diesel locomotives, class numbers offer an indication of engine horsepower as shown in the table below.

Class No. Range	Engine hp
01–14	0–799
15–20	800–1000
21–31	1001–1499
32–39	1500–1999
40–54, 57	2000–2999
55–56, 58–70	3000+

For electric locomotives class numbers are allocated in ascending numerical order under the following scheme:

Class 71–79   Direct current and DC/diesel dual system locomotives.
Class 81 onwards   Alternating current and AC/DC dual system locomotives.

Numbers in the 891xx to 899xx series are allocated to locomotives which have been deregistered but subsequently re-registered for use on the national railway network and whose original number has already been reused. 89xxx numbers are normally only carried inside locomotive cabs and are not carried externally in normal circumstances.

WHEEL ARRANGEMENT

For main line locomotives the number of driven axles on a bogie or frame is denoted by a letter (A = 1, B = 2, C = 3 etc) and the number of non-powered axles is denoted by a number. The use of the letter "o" after a letter indicates each axle is individually powered, whilst the "+" symbol indicates bogies are inter-coupled.

For shunting locomotives, the Whyte notation is used. In this notation the number of leading wheels are given, followed by the number of driving wheels and then the trailing wheels.

UNITS OF MEASUREMENT

All dimensions and weights are quoted for locomotives in an "as new" condition with all necessary supplies (eg oil, water and sand) on board. Dimensions are quoted in the order length x width. Lengths quoted are over buffers or couplers as appropriate. All widths quoted are maxima. Where two different wheel diameter dimensions are shown, the first refers to powered wheels and the second refers to non-powered wheels. All weights are shown as metric tonnes (t = tonnes).

HAULAGE CAPABILITY OF DIESEL LOCOMOTIVES

The haulage capability of a diesel locomotive depends upon three basic factors:

1. Adhesive weight. The greater the weight on the driving wheels, the greater the adhesion and more tractive power can be applied before wheelslip occurs.

2. The characteristics of its transmission. To start a train the locomotive has to exert a pull at standstill. A direct drive diesel engine cannot do this, hence the need for transmission. This may be mechanical, hydraulic or electric. The present British Standard for locomotives is electric transmission. Here the diesel engine drives a generator or alternator and the current produced is fed to the traction motors. The force produced by each driven wheel depends on the current in its traction motor. In other words, the larger the current, the harder it pulls. As the locomotive speed increases, the current in the traction motor falls, hence the *Maximum Tractive Effort* is the maximum force at its wheels the locomotive can exert at a standstill. The electrical equipment cannot take such high currents for long without overheating. Hence the *Continuous Tractive Effort* is quoted which represents the current which the equipment can take continuously.

3. The power of its engine. Not all power reaches the rail, as electrical machines are approximately 90% efficient. As the electrical energy passes through two such machines (the generator or alternator and the traction motors), the *Power at Rail* is approximately 81% (90% of 90%) of the engine power, less a further amount used for auxiliary equipment such as radiator fans, traction motor blowers, air compressors, battery charging, cab heating, Electric Train Supply (ETS) etc. The power of the locomotive is proportional to the tractive effort times the speed. Hence when on full power there is a speed corresponding to the continuous tractive effort.

HAULAGE CAPABILITY OF ELECTRIC LOCOMOTIVES

Unlike a diesel locomotive, an electric locomotive does not develop its power on board and its performance is determined only by two factors, namely its weight and the characteristics of its electrical equipment. Whereas a diesel locomotive tends to be a constant power machine, the power of an electric locomotive varies considerably. Up to a certain speed it can produce virtually a constant tractive effort. Hence power rises with speed according to the formula given in section three above, until a maximum speed is reached at which tractive effort falls, such that the power also falls. Hence the power at the speed corresponding to the maximum tractive effort is lower than the maximum speed.

BRAKE FORCE

Brake Force (also known as brake power) is a measure of the braking power of a locomotive. The Brake Force available is dependant on the adhesion between the rail and the wheels being braked and the normal reaction of the rail on the wheels being braked (and hence on the weight per braked wheel). A locomotive's Brake Force is shown on its data panels so operating staff can ensure sufficient brake power is available for specific trains.

ELECTRIC TRAIN SUPPLY (ETS)

A number of locomotives are equipped to provide a supply of electricity to the train being hauled to power auxiliaries such as heating, cooling fans, air conditioning and kitchen equipment. ETS is provided from the locomotive by means of a separate alternator (except Class 33 locomotives, which have a DC generator). The ETS index of a locomotive is a measure of the electrical power available for train supply. Class 55 locomotives provide an ETS directly from one of their traction generators into the train supply.

Similarly, most locomotive-hauled carriages also have an ETS index, which in this case is a measure of the power required to operate equipment mounted in the carriage. The sum of the ETS indices of all the hauled vehicles in a train must not exceed the ETS index of the locomotive.

ETS is commonly (but incorrectly) known as ETH (Electric Train Heating), which is a throwback to the days before locomotive-hauled carriages were equipped with electrically powered auxiliary equipment other than for train heating.

ROUTE AVAILABILITY (RA)

This is a measure of a railway vehicle's axle load. The higher the axle load of a vehicle, the higher the RA number on a scale from 1 to 10. Each Network Rail route has a RA number and in general no vehicle with a higher RA number may travel on that route without special clearance.

MULTIPLE WORKING

Multiple working between vehicles (ie two or more powered vehicles being driven from one cab) is facilitated by jumper cables connecting the vehicles. However, not all types of locomotive are compatible with each other, and a number of different systems are in use. Some are compatible with others, some are not. BR used "multiple working codes" to designate which locomotives were compatible. The list below shows which classes of locomotives are compatible with each other – the former BR multiple working code being shown in brackets. It should be noted that some locomotives have had the equipment removed or made inoperable.

With other classes:
Classes 20, 25, 31, 33, 37 40 & 73/1*. (Blue Star)
Classes 56 & 58. (Red Diamond)
Classes 59, 66, 67, 68, 70, 73/9 & 88.
* DRS has since adapted the systems so its Classes 20/3, 37, 47 & 57 can work with each other only.

With other members of same class only:
Class 43, Class 47 (Green Circle), Class 50 (Orange Square), Class 60.

PUSH-PULL OPERATION

Some locomotives are modified to operate passenger and service (formed of laboratory, test and inspection carriages) trains in "push-pull" mode – which allows the train to be driven from either end – either with locomotives at each end (both under power) or with a driving brake van at one end and a locomotive at the other. Various different systems are now in use. Electric locomotive Classes 86, 87, 90 & 91 use a time-division multiplex (TDM) system for push-pull working which utilises the existing Railway Clearing House (RCH) jumper cables fitted to carriages. Previously these cables had only been used to control train lighting and public address systems.

More recently locomotives of Classes 67 and 68 have used the Association of American Railroads (AAR) system.

ABBREVIATIONS

Standard abbreviations used in this section of the book are:

a   Train air brake equipment only.
b   Drophead buckeye couplers.
c   Scharfenberg couplers.
d   Fitted with retractable Dellner couplers.
e   European Railway Traffic Management System (ERTMS) signalling equipment fitted.
k   Fitted with Swinghead Automatic "buckeye" combination couplers.
p   Train air, vacuum and electro-pneumatic brakes.
r   Radio Electric Token Block signalling equipment fitted.
s   Slow Speed Control equipment.
v   Train vacuum brake only.
x   Train air and vacuum brakes ("Dual brakes").
+   Additional fuel tank capacity.
§   Sandite laying equipment.

In all cases use of the above abbreviations indicates the equipment in question is normally operable. The definition of non-standard abbreviations and symbols is detailed in individual class headings.

▲ BR Green-liveried 08925 shunts March Whitemoor yard on 29/03/18.
Peter Foster

▼ Revised Direct Rail Services-liveried 20303 and 20305 top-and-tail a Railhead Treatment Train at Sheffield on 02/10/18, bound for Gainsborough Trent Junction.　　**Robert Pritchard**

▲ West Coast Railway Company maroon-liveried 33029 and 57316 top-and-tail the 14.40 Oxenholme Lake District–Windermere through Burneside on 22/06/18. **Anthony Hicks**

▲ BR Revised blue-liveried 37424 (also carrying the number 37558) leaves Kirkby-in-Furness with the 08.42 Barrow-in-Furness–Carlisle on 03/06/17. **Andrew Mason**

▲ Europhoenix-liveried 37800 approaches Swanley on 05/05/18 hauling Electrostar 375 307 from Derby to Ramsgate. **Brian Carter**

▼ BR Green-liveried D213 (40013) departs Scarborough with a Saphos Trains railtour returning to Crewe on 06/10/18. **Andrew Mason**

▲ Great Western Railway Green-liveried 43188 and 43194 with short set GW01 are seen at Powderham on 31/08/18 with the 09.26 Exeter St Davids–Penzance. **Tony Christie**

▲ ScotRail InterCity-liveried 43033 and 43183 pass Dalgety Bay with the 09.38 Haymarket–Dundee crew training run on 15/09/18. **Ian Lothian**

▼ Caledonian Sleeper-liveried 47727 passes Worcester Shrub Hill with a Gloucester to Burton-upon-Trent empty stock working on 15/07/18.
Dave Gommersall

▲ BR Blue-liveried D9009 (55009) stands at London King's Cross after arrival with "The Talisman" railtour from Newcastle on 15/09/18. **Mark Beal**

▼ Colas Rail-liveried 56078 waits in Heeley loop, Sheffield with 6Z56 13.15 York Thrall–Shrewsbury train of RHTT sets on 31/08/18. **Robert Pritchard**

▲ West Coast Railway Company-liveried 57313 passes Longport with a 17.50 Nottingham–Carnforth (Northern Belle stock) on 03/06/18 **Cliff Beeton**

▼ Hanson-liveried 59101 passes Gatwick Airport with 7O69 12.34 Acton–Crawley New Yard aggregates train on 15/02/18. **Alex Dasi-Sutton**

1.1. DIESEL SHUNTING LOCOMOTIVES

All BR design shunting locomotives still in existence, apart from those considered to be preserved, are now listed together in this section. Preserved shunting locomotives are listed in the Platform 5 publication "Preserved Locomotives of British Railways" (a small number are listed in both that book and in this publication).

Few shunting locomotives have engineering acceptance and are equipped to operate on Network Rail infrastructure (beyond interface infrastructure), but those that are known to be permitted are indicated here.

For shunting locomotives, instead of the two-letter depot code, actual locations at the time of publication are given. Pool codes for shunting locomotives are not shown.

CLASS 03   BR/GARDNER   0-6-0

Built: 1958–62 by BR at Swindon or Doncaster Works.
Engine: Gardner 8L3 of 152 kW (204 hp) at 1200 rpm.
Transmission: Mechanical. Fluidrive type 23 hydraulic coupling to Wilson-Drewry CA5R7 gearbox with SCG type RF11 final drive.
Maximum Tractive Effort: 68 kN (15300 lbf).
Continuous Tractive Effort: 68 kN (15300 lbf) at 3.75 mph.
Train Brakes: Air & vacuum.

Brake Force: 13 t.	**Dimensions:** 7.93 x 2.59 m.
Weight: 31.3 t.	**Wheel Diameter:** 1092 mm.
Design Speed: 28.5 mph.	**Maximum Speed:** 28.5 mph.
Fuel Capacity: 1364 litres.	**Route Availability:** 1.
Train Supply: Not equipped.	**Total:** 3.

Number Notes Livery Owner Location

Number	Notes	Livery	Owner	Location
03084		G	WC	West Coast Railway Company, Carnforth Depot
03196		B	WC	West Coast Railway Company, Carnforth Depot
D2381	v	G	WC	West Coast Railway Company, Carnforth Depot

CLASS 07   BR/RUSTON & HORNSBY   0-6-0

Built: 1962 by Ruston & Hornsby, Lincoln.
Engine: Paxman 6RPHL Mk III of 205 kW (275 hp) at 1360 rpm.
Transmission: Electric. One AEI RTB 6652 traction motor.
Maximum Tractive Effort: 126 kN (28240 lbf).
Continuous Tractive Effort: 71 kN (15950 lbf) at 4.38 mph.
Train Brakes: Vacuum.

Brake Force:	**Dimensions:** 8.17 x 2.59 m.
Weight: 43.6 t.	**Wheel Diameter:** 1067 mm.
Design Speed: 20 mph.	**Maximum Speed:** 20 mph.
Fuel Capacity: 1400 litres.	**Train Supply:** Not equipped.
Total: 1.	

07007	v	B	AF	Arlington Fleet Services, Eastleigh Works, Hants

CLASS 08   BR/ENGLISH ELECTRIC   0-6-0

Built: 1955–62 by BR at Crewe, Darlington, Derby Locomotive, Doncaster or Horwich Works.
Engine: English Electric 6KT of 298 kW (400 hp) at 680 rpm.
Main Generator: English Electric 801.
Traction Motors: Two English Electric 506.
Maximum Tractive Effort: 156 kN (35000 lbf).
Continuous Tractive Effort: 49 kN (11100 lbf) at 8.8 mph.

Power at Rail: 194 kW (260 hp).	**Train Brakes:** Air & vacuum.
Brake Force: 19 t.	**Dimensions:** 8.92 x 2.59 m.
Weight: 49.6–50.4 t.	**Wheel Diameter:** 1372 mm.
Design Speed: 20 mph.	**Maximum Speed:** 15 mph.
Fuel Capacity: 3037 litres.	**Route Availability:** 5.
Train Supply: Not equipped.	**Total:** 168.

* Locomotives with engineering acceptence to operate on Network Rail infrastructure. 08850 has acceptance for use between Battersby and Whitby only, for rescue purposes.

† – Fitted with remote control equipment.

§ – On hire from Nottingham Transport Heritage Centre.

Non-standard liveries:

08308	All over ScotRail Caledonian Sleeper purple.
08401	Dark green.
08423	Dark blue.
08442	Dark grey lower bodyside & light grey upper bodyside.
08445	Yellow, blue & green.
08447	Lilac.
08502	Mid blue.
08568	Dark grey lower bodyside & light grey upper bodyside. Red solebar stripe.
08598	Yellow.
08600	Red with a light grey roof.
08682	Multi-coloured.
08774	Red.
08823	Yellow, blue & green.
08870	Light grey.
08899	Crimson lake.
08913	Yellow, blue & green.
08956	Serco Railtest blue.

Number	Notes	Livery	Owner	Location
08220	v	**B**	RS	EMD, Longport Works, Stoke-on-Trent, Staffs§
08308	a	**0**	RL	Weardale Railway, Wolsingham, County Durham
08331		**K**	20	Midland Railway-Butterley, Derbyshire
08375	a	**K**	RL	Hanson Cement, Ketton Cement Works, nr Stamford
08389	a†	**E**	HN	Celsa Steel UK, Tremorfa Steelworks, Cardiff
08401	a	**0**	HU	Hams Hall Distribution Park, Coleshill, Warwickshire
08405	a†	**E**	RS	East Midlands Trains, Neville Hill Depot, Leeds
08410	* a	**GW**	GW	Great Western Railway, Long Rock Depot, Penzance

08411	a	B	RS	RSS, Rye Farm, Wishaw, Sutton Coldfield (S)
08417	* a	Y	NR	Loram (UK), RTC Business Park, Derby
08418	a	E	WC	West Coast Railway Company, Carnforth Depot
08423	a	O	RL	PD Ports, Teesport, Grangetown, Middlesbrough
08428	ak	E	HN	Barrow Hill Roundhouse, Chesterfield, Derbys (S)
08441	* a	RS	RS	LNER, Bounds Green Depot, London
08442	a	O	AV	Arriva TrainCare, Eastleigh Depot, Hampshire (S)
08445	a	O	HU	Daventry International Railfreight Terminal, Crick
08447	a	O	RU	John G Russell (Transport), Hillington, Glasgow (S)
08451	*	B	AM	Alstom, Longsight Depot, Manchester
08454	*	B	AM	Alstom, Widnes Technology Centre, Merseyside
08460	a	RS	RS	Axiom Rail, Stoke-on-Trent Works, Staffordshire
08472	* a	WA	WA	LNER, Craigentinny Depot, Edinburgh
08480	a	RS	RS	Greater Anglia, Crown Point Depot, Norwich
08483	* a	K	GW	Great Western Railway, Laira Depot, Plymouth
08484	a	RS	RS	Hitachi Rail Europe, Newton Aycliffe, Co Durham
08485	a	B	WC	West Coast Railway Company, Carnforth Depot
08499	a	B	CS	Colas Rail, Canton Depot, Cardiff
08500		E	HN	Nemesis Rail, Burton-upon-Trent, Staffordshire (S)
08502		O	HN	GB Railfreight, Garston Car Terminal, Liverpool
08503	a	B	RS	Barry Rail Centre, Vale of Glamorgan
08507	a	RB	RV	Nemesis Rail, Burton-upon-Trent, Staffordshire
08511	a	RS	RS	Arriva TrainCare, Cambridge Depot
08516	a	LW	AV	Arriva TrainCare, Barton Hill Depot, Bristol
08523	*	B	RL	ScotRail, Inverness Depot
08525		ST	EM	East Midlands Trains, Neville Hill Depot, Leeds
08527		FA	HN	GB Railfreight, Inter Terminals, Immingham East Dock
08530	*	FL	FL	Freightliner, Southampton Maritime FLT
08531	* a	FH	FL	LH Group, Barton-under-Needwood, Staffordshire
08536		B	RS	RSS, Rye Farm, Wishaw, Sutton Coldfield (S)
08567		E	AF	Arlington Fleet Services, Eastleigh Works, Hants
08568	a	O	RS	RSS, Rye Farm, Wishaw, Sutton Coldfield (S)
08571	* a	WA	WA	Daventry International Railfreight Terminal, Crick
08573		K	RL	Weardale Railway, Wolsingham, County Durham
08575		FL	FL	Nemesis Rail, Burton-upon-Trent, Staffordshire (S)
08578		E	HN	Quinton Rail Technology Centre, Long Marston, Warks (S)
08580	*	RS	RS	LNER, Bounds Green Depot, London
08585	*	FH	FL	Freightliner, Southampton Maritime FLT
08588		RL	RL	Loram (UK), RTC Business Park, Derby
08593		E	RS	RSS, Rye Farm, Wishaw, Sutton Coldfield (S)
08596	* a†	WA	WA	LNER, Craigentinny Depot, Edinburgh
08598		O	AD	AV Dawson, Ayrton Rail Terminal, Middlesbrough
08600	a	O	AD	AV Dawson, Ayrton Rail Terminal, Middlesbrough
08602		B	BT	Bombardier Transportation, Derby Works
08605	†	DB	RV	Ecclesbourne Valley Railway, Wirksworth, Derbyshire
08611	*	B	AM	Alstom, Wembley Depot, London
08613		RL	RL	PD Ports, Teesport, Grangetown, Middlesbrough
08615	*	WA	WA	LH Group, Barton-under-Needwood, Staffordshire
08616		LM	WM	West Midlands Trains, Tyseley Depot, Birmingham
08617	*	B	AM	Alstom, Oxley Depot, Wolverhampton
08622		K	RL	Hanson Cement, Ketton Cement Works, nr Stamford

08623		DB	HN	Hope Cement, Hope Cement Works, Derbys (S)
08624	*	FH	FL	Freightliner, Felixstowe FLT
08629		KB	KB	Knorr-Bremse Rail UK, Wolverton Works, Milton Keynes
08630	†	K	HN	Celsa Steel UK, Tremorfa Steelworks, Cardiff
08632	†	RS	RS	East Midlands Trains, Neville Hill Depot, Leeds
08641	*	B	GW	Great Western Railway, Laira Depot, Plymouth
08643		B	MR	Aggregate Industries, Merehead Rail Terminal
08644	*	B	GW	Great Western Railway, Laira Depot, Plymouth
08645	*	DG	GW	Great Western Railway, Landore Depot, Swansea
08648		K	RL	ScotRail, Inverness Depot
08649		KB	KB	Knorr-Bremse Rail UK, Wolverton Works, Milton Keynes
08650		B	MR	Hanson Aggregates, Whatley Quarry, near Frome
08652		B	MR	Aggregate Industries, Merehead Rail Terminal
08653		E	HN	Quinton Rail Technology Centre, Long Marston, Warks (S)
08663	* a	B	GW	Great Western Railway, St Philip's Marsh Depot, Bristol
08669	* a	WA	WA	Wabtec Rail, Doncaster Works
08670	* a	RS	RS	LNER, Bounds Green Depot, London
08676		E	HN	East Kent Light Railway, Shepherdswell, Kent (S)
08678	a	WC	WC	West Coast Railway Company, Carnforth Depot
08682		O	BT	Bombardier Transportation, Derby Works
08683		RS	RS	Greater Anglia, Crown Point Depot, Norwich
08685		E	HN	East Kent Light Railway, Shepherdswell, Kent (S)
08690		ST	EM	East Midlands Trains, Neville Hill Depot, Leeds (S)
08691	*	FL	FL	Freightliner, Felixstowe FLT
08696	* a	B	AM	Alstom, Wembley Depot, London
08700		B	HN	Bombardier Transportation, Ilford Works, London
08701	a	RX	HN	Quinton Rail Technology Centre, Long Marston, Warks (S)
08703	a	E	RS	DB Cargo UK, Springs Branch Depot, Wigan
08704		RB	RV	Ecclesbourne Valley Railway
08706	†	E	HN	RSS, Rye Farm, Wishaw, Sutton Coldfield (S)
08709		E	HN	RSS, Rye Farm, Wishaw, Sutton Coldfield (S)
08711	k	RX	HN	Nemesis Rail, Burton-upon-Trent, Staffordshire (S)
08714		E	HN	Hope Cement, Hope Cement Works, Derbys (S)
08721	*	B	AM	Alstom, Widnes Technology Centre, Merseyside
08724	*	WA	WA	Wabtec Rail, Doncaster Works
08730		KB	KB	Knorr-Bremse Rail UK, Springburn Depot, Glasgow
08735	†	E	AV	Arriva TrainCare, Eastleigh Depot, Hampshire (S)
08738		FER	RS	RSS, Rye Farm, Wishaw, Sutton Coldfield (S)
08742	†	RX	HN	East Kent Light Railway, Shepherdswell, Kent (S)
08743		B	SU	SembCorp Utilities UK, Wilton, Middlesbrough
08750	a	K	RL	Weardale Railway, Wolsingham, County Durham (S)
08752	†	E	RS	RSS, Rye Farm, Wishaw, Sutton Coldfield (S)
08754	*	B	RL	Weardale Railway, Wolsingham, County Durham
08756		DG	RL	Weardale Railway, Wolsingham, County Durham
08762		K	RL	Weardale Railway, Wolsingham, County Durham
08764	*	B	AM	Alstom, Polmadie Depot, Glasgow
08765		HN	HN	Barrow Hill Roundhouse, Chesterfield, Derbys (S)
08774	a	O	AD	AV Dawson, Ayrton Rail Terminal, Middlesbrough
08782	a†	CU	HN	Barrow HIll Roundhouse, Chesterfield, Derbys (S)
08783		E	ER	European Metal Recycling, Kingsbury, nr Tamworth
08785	* a	FL	FL	Freightliner, Trafford Park FLT

08786	a	DG	HN	Barrow Hill Roundhouse, Chesterfield, Derbys (S)
08787		B	MR	Hanson Aggregates, Machen Quarry, near Newport
08788	*	RL	RL	Tata Steel, Shotton Works, Deeside
08790	*	B	AM	Alstom, Edge Hill Depot, Liverpool
08795	*	K	GW	Great Western Railway, Landore Depot, Swansea
08798		E	ER	European Metal Recycling, Attercliffe, Sheffield
08799	a	E	HN	East Kent Light Railway, Shepherdswell, Kent (S)
08802	†	RX	HN	RSS, Rye Farm, Wishaw, Sutton Coldfield (S)
08804	†	E	HN	East Kent Light Railway, Shepherdswell, Kent (S)
08805		FO	WM	West Midlands Trains, Soho Depot, Birmingham
08809		RL	RL	Weardale Railway, Wolsingham, County Durham
08810	a	LW	AV	Arriva TrainCare, Eastleigh Depot, Hampshire
08818		GB	HN	GB Railfreight, Garston Car Terminal, Liverpool
08822	*	IC	GW	Great Western Railway, St Philip's Marsh Depot, Bristol
08823	a	O	HU	LH Group, Barton-under-Needwood, Staffordshire (S)
08824	ak	K	HN	Barrow HIll Roundhouse, Chesterfield, Derbys (S)
08834		HN	HN	Northern, Allerton Depot, Liverpool
08836	*	GW	GW	Great Western Railway, Reading Depot
08846		B	RS	RSS, Rye Farm, Wishaw, Sutton Coldfield
08847	*	CD	RL	Mid Norfolk Railway, East Dereham, Norfolk
08850	*	B	NY	North Yorkshire Moors Railway, Grosmont Depot
08853	* a	WA	WA	Wabtec Rail, Doncaster Works
08865		E	HN	Hope Cement, Hope Cement Works, Derbys (S)
08868		AW	HN	Arriva TrainCare, Crewe Depot, Cheshire
08870		O	RL	Weardale Railway, Wolsingham, County Durham
08871		CD	RL	Bombardier Transportation, Ilford Works, London
08872		E	ER	European Metal Recycling, Attercliffe, Sheffield
08873	*	RX	HU	LH Group, Barton-under-Needwood, Staffordshire (S)
08874	*	SL	RL	Weardale Railway, Wolsingham, County Durham
08877		DG	HN	Barrow Hill Roundhouse, Chesterfield, Derbys (S)
08879		E	HN	Barrow Hill Roundhouse, Chesterfield, Derbys (S)
08885		B	RL	Weardale Railway, Wolsingham, County Durham (S)
08887	* a	B	AM	Alstom, Polmadie Depot, Glasgow
08891	*	FL	FL	Nemesis Rail, Burton-upon-Trent, Staffordshire (S)
08892		DR	HN	Bombardier Transportation, Old Dalby Test Centre, Asfordby
08899		O	EM	East Midlands Trains, Derby Etches Park Depot
08903		B	SU	SembCorp Utilities UK, Wilton, Middlesbrough
08904		E	HN	Celsa Steel UK, Tremorfa Steelworks, Cardiff
08905		E	HN	Hope Cement, Hope Cement Works, Derbys (S)
08908		ST	EM	East Midlands Trains, Neville Hill Depot, Leeds (S)
08912		B	AD	AV Dawson, Ayrton Rail Terminal, Middlesbrough (S)
08918		DG	HN	Nemesis Rail, Burton-upon-Trent, Staffordshire (S)
08921		E	HN	European Metal Recycling, Kingsbury, nr Tamworth
08924	†	GB	HN	Celsa Steel UK, Tremorfa Steelworks, Cardiff
08925		G	GB	GB Railfreight, Whitemoor Yard, March, Cambs
08927		G	RS	RSS, Rye Farm, Wishaw, Sutton Coldfield
08933		B	MR	Aggregate Industries, Merehead Rail Terminal
08934	a	VP	GB	GB Railfreight, Dagenham Car Terminal, Essex
08936		B	RL	Weardale Railway, Wolsingham, County Durham
08937		G	BD	Dartmoor Railway, Meldon Quarry, nr Okehampton
08939		FER	RS	RSS, Rye Farm, Wishaw, Sutton Coldfield (S)

08943		**HN**	HN	Bombardier Transportation, Central Rivers Depot, Barton-under-Needwood
08947		**B**	MR	Hanson Aggregates, Whatley Quarry, near Frome
08948	c	**EP**	EU	Eurostar, Temple Mills Depot, London
08950		**ST**	EM	East Midlands Trains, Neville Hill Depot, Leeds (S)
08954	*	**B**	AM	Alstom, Polmadie Depot, Glasgow
08956		**0**	LO	Bombardier Transportation, Old Dalby Test Centre, Asfordby

Class 08/9. Reduced height cab. Converted 1985–87 by BR at Landore.

| 08994 | a | **E** | HN | Nemesis Rail, Burton-upon-Trent, Staffordshire (S) |

Other numbers or names carried:

08308	"23"	08682	Lionheart
08375	"21"	08690	DAVID THIRKILL
08423	"H011" / "14"	08691	Terri
08451	LONGSIGHT TMD	08743	Bryan Turner
08460	SPIRIT OF THE OAK	08754	"H041"
08484	CAPTAIN NATHANIEL DARELL	08774	ARTHUR VERNON DAWSON
08499	REDLIGHT	08787	"08296"
08525	DUNCAN BEDFORD	08790	M.A. SMITH
08568	St. Rollox	08809	"24"
08585	Vicky	08810	RICHARD J. WENHAM
08588	"H047"		EASTLEIGH DEPOT
08602	"004"		DECEMBER 1989 – JULY 1999
08605	"WIGAN2"	08818	MOLLY / "CELSA 4"
08613	"H064"	08822	Dave Mills
08616	TYSELEY 100 / 3783	08823	LIBBIE
08617	Steve Purser	08824	"IEMD 01"
08622	"H028" / "19"	08846	"003"
08624	Rambo PAUL RAMSEY	08870	"H024"
08629	Wolverton	08871	"H074"
08630	Celsa Endeavour /"CELSA 3"	08874	Catherine
08641	Pride of Laira	08885	"H042" / "18"
08644	Laira Diesel Depot	08899	Midland Counties Railway
	50 Years 1962–2012		175 1839–2014
08645	Mike Baggott	08903	John W Antill
08649	Bradwell	08924	"CELSA 2"
08663	St. Silas	08927	D4157
08669	Bob Machin	08937	D4167
08678	"555"	08950	DAVID LIGHTFOOT

CLASS 09   BR/ENGLISH ELECTRIC   0-6-0

Built: 1959–62 by BR at Darlington or Horwich Works.
Engine: English Electric 6KT of 298 kW (400 hp) at 680 rpm.
Main Generator: English Electric 801.
Traction Motors: English Electric 506.
Maximum Tractive Effort: 111 kN (25000 lbf).
Continuous Tractive Effort: 39 kN (8800 lbf) at 11.6 mph.
Power at Rail: 201 kW (269 hp).   **Train Brakes:** Air & vacuum.
Brake Force: 19 t.   **Dimensions:** 8.92 x 2.59 m.

Weight: 49 t.		**Wheel Diameter:** 1372 mm.	
Design Speed: 27 mph.		**Maximum Speed:** 27 mph.	
Fuel Capacity: 3037 litres.		**Route Availability:** 5.	
Train Supply: Not equipped.		**Total:** 11.	

Class 09/0. Built as Class 09.

09002	**G**	GB	GB Railfreight, Whitemoor Yard, March, Cambs
09006	**E**	HN	Nemesis Rail, Burton-upon-Trent, Staffordshire (S)
09007	**G**	LN	London Overground, Willesden Depot, London
09009	**G**	GB	Miles Platting Stone Terminal, Greater Manchester
09014	**DG**	HN	Nemesis Rail, Burton-upon-Trent, Staffordshire (S)
09015	**E**	RS	RSS, Rye Farm, Wishaw, Sutton Coldfield (S)
09022	**B**	VG	Victoria Group, Port of Boston, Boston
09023	**E**	ER	European Metal Recycling, Attercliffe, Sheffield

Class 09/1. Converted from Class 08 1992–93 by RFS Industries, Kilnhurst. 110 V electrical equipment.

09106	**HN**	HN	Barrow HIll Roundhouse, Chesterfield, Derbys

Class 09/2. Converted from Class 08 1992 by RFS Industries, Kilnhurst. 90 V electrical equipment.

09201	**DG**	HN	Hope Cement, Hope Cement Works, Derbys (S)
09204	**AW**	AV	Arriva TrainCare, Crewe Depot, Cheshire

Other numbers or names carried:

09007	D3671	09106	"6"

1.2. MAIN LINE DIESEL LOCOMOTIVES

CLASS 19

Experimental locomotive being rebuilt by Artemis Intelligent Power from a Mark 3B Driving Brake Van. Part of a project funded by the Rail Safety & Standards Board (RSSB) to test the viability of combining hydrostatic transmission to reduce engine emissions. Conversion work is taking place at the Bo'ness & Kinneil Railway. Full details awaited.

Built: 1988 by BR Derby Works.
Engine: 2 x JCB diesel engines.
Main Generator:
Traction Motors:
Maximum Tractive Effort:

Continuous Tractive Effort:	**Train Brakes:**
Power at Rail:	**Dimensions:** 18.83 x 2.71 m.
Brake Force:	**Weight:**
Design Speed:	**Maximum Speed:**
Fuel Capacity:	**Route Availability:**
Train Supply:	**Total:** 1.

19001	(82113)	**B**	AV	BO

CLASS 20   ENGLISH ELECTRIC   Bo-Bo

Built: 1957–68 by English Electric at Vulcan Foundry, Newton-le-Willows or by Robert Stephenson & Hawthorns at Darlington.
Engine: English Electric 8SVT Mk II of 746 kW (1000 hp) at 850 rpm.
Main Generator: English Electric 819/3C.
Traction Motors: English Electric 526/5D or 526/8D.
Maximum Tractive Effort: 187 kN (42000 lbf).
Continuous Tractive Effort: 111 kN (25000 lbf) at 11 mph.

Power at Rail: 574 kW (770 hp).	**Train Brakes:** Air & vacuum.
Brake Force: 35 t.	**Dimensions:** 14.25 x 2.67 m.
Weight: 73.4–73.5 t.	**Wheel Diameter:** 1092 mm.
Design Speed: 75 mph.	**Maximum Speed:** 75 mph.
Fuel Capacity: 1727 litres.	**Route Availability:** 5.
Train Supply: Not equipped.	**Total:** 33.

Non-standard liveries/numbering:

20056 Yellow with grey cabsides and red solebar. Carries No. "81".
20066 Dark blue with yellow stripes. Carries No. "82".
20088 RFS grey. Carries No. 2017.
20110 Carries original number D8110.
20142 LUL Maroon.
20168 White with green cabsides and solebar. Carries No. "2".
20227 LUL Maroon.
20906 White. Carries No. "3".

Class 20/0. Standard Design.

20007	**G**	20	MOLO	SK
20016	**B**	HN	HNRS	LM (S)
20056	**O**	HN	HNRL	SC
20066	**O**	HN	HNRL	HO
20081	**B**	HN	HNRS	LM (S)
20088	**O**	HN	HNRS	LM (S)
20096	**B**	HN	GBEE	BH	Ian Goddard 1938–2016
20107	**B**	HN	GBEE	BH
20110	**G**	HN	HNRS	BQ (S)
20118	**FO**	HN	GBEE	BH	Saltburn-by-the-Sea
20121	**HN**	HN	HNRL	BH (S)
20132	**FO**	HN	GBEE	BH	Barrow Hill Depot
20142	**O**	20	MOLO	SK	SIR JOHN BETJEMAN
20166	**HN**	HN	HNRL	Leeming Bar
20168	**O**	HN	HNRL	HO	SIR GEORGE EARLE
20189	**B**	20	MOLO	SK
20205	**B**	2L	MOLO	SK
20227	**O**	2L	MOLO	SK	SHERLOCK HOLMES

Class 20/3. Direct Rail Services refurbished locomotives. Details as Class 20/0 except:

Refurbished: 15 locomotives were refurbished 1995–96 by Brush Traction at Loughborough (20301–305) or 1997–98 by RFS(E) at Doncaster (20306–315). Disc indicators or headcode panels removed.

Train Brakes: Air.   **Maximum Speed:** 60 mph (+ 75 mph).
Weight: 73 t (+ 76 t).   **Fuel Capacity:** 2909 (+ 4909) litres.
Brake Force: 35 t (+ 31 t).   **RA:** 5 (+ 6).

20301	(20047)	r	**DS** DR XHSS	BH (S)	
20302	(20084)	r	**DS** DR XHNC	KM	
20303	(20127)	r	**DS** DR XHNC	KM	Max Joule 1958–1999
20304	(20120)	r	**DS** DR XHSS	BH (S)	
20305	(20095)	r	**DS** DR XHNC	KM	
20308	(20187)	r+	**DS** DR XHSS	BH (S)	
20309	(20075)	r+	**DS** DR XHSS	BH (S)	
20311	(20102)	r+	**HN** HN GBEE	BH	
20312	(20042)	r+	**DS** DR XHSS	BH (S)	
20314	(20117)	r+	**HN** HN GBEE	BH	

Class 20/9. Harry Needle Railroad Company (former Hunslet-Barclay/ DRS) locomotives. Details as Class 20/0 except:

Refurbished: 1989 by Hunslet-Barclay at Kilmarnock.
Train Brakes: Air.   **Fuel Capacity:** 1727 (+ 4727) litres.
RA: 5 (+ 6).

20901	(20101)		**GB** HN GBEE	BH
20903	(20083)	+	**DR** HN HNRS	BU (S)
20904	(20041)		**DR** HN HNRS	BU (S)
20905	(20225)	+	**GB** HN GBEE	BH
20906	(20219)		**O** HN HNRL	HO

CLASS 25   BR/BEYER PEACOCK/SULZER   Bo-Bo

Built: 1965 by Beyer Peacock at Gorton.
Engine: Sulzer 6LDA28-B of 930 kW (1250 hp) at 750 rpm.
Main Generator: AEI RTB15656.   **Traction Motors:** AEI 253AY.
Maximum Tractive Effort: 200 kN (45000 lbf).
Continuous Tractive Effort: 93 kN (20800 lbf) at 17.1 mph.
Power at Rail: 708 kW (949 hp).   **Train Brakes:** Air & vacuum.
Brake Force: 38 t.   **Dimensions:** 15.39 x 2.73 m.
Weight: 71.5 t.   **Wheel Diameter:** 1143 mm.
Design Speed: 90 mph.   **Maximum Speed:** 60 mph.
Fuel Capacity: 2270 litres.   **Route Availability:** 5.
Train Supply: Not equipped.   **Total:** 1.

Carries original number D7628.

Only certified for use on Network Rail tracks between Whitby and Battersby, as an extension of North Yorkshire Moors Railway services.

25278	**GG** NY MBDL		NY	SYBILLA

CLASS 31   BRUSH/ENGLISH ELECTRIC   A1A-A1A

Built: 1958–62 by Brush Traction at Loughborough.
Engine: English Electric 12SVT of 1100 kW (1470 hp) at 850 rpm.
Main Generator: Brush TG160-48.   **Traction Motors:** Brush TM73-68.
Maximum Tractive Effort: 160 kN (35900 lbf).
Continuous Tractive Effort: 83 kN (18700 lbf) at 23.5 mph.

Power at Rail: 872 kW (1170 hp).	**Train Brakes:** Air & vacuum.
Brake Force: 49 t.	**Dimensions:** 17.30 x 2.67 m.
Weight: 106.7–111 t.	**Wheel Diameter:** 1092/1003 mm.
Design Speed: 90 mph.	**Maximum Speed:** 90 mph.
Fuel Capacity: 2409 litres.	**Route Availability:** 5 or 6.
Train Supply: Not equipped.	**Total:** 2.

Class 31/1. Standard Design. RA: 5.

31105	**Y**	NR	QADD	ZA (S)	
31233 a	**Y**	NR	QADD	ZA (S)	

CLASS 33   BRCW/SULZER   Bo-Bo

Built: 1960–62 by the Birmingham Railway Carriage & Wagon Company at Smethwick.
Engine: Sulzer 8LDA28 of 1160 kW (1550 hp) at 750 rpm.
Main Generator: Crompton Parkinson CG391B1.
Traction Motors: Crompton Parkinson C171C2.
Maximum Tractive Effort: 200 kN (45000 lbf).
Continuous Tractive Effort: 116 kN (26000 lbf) at 17.5 mph.

Power at Rail: 906 kW (1215 hp).	**Train Brakes:** Air & vacuum.
Brake Force: 35 t.	**Dimensions:** 15.47 x 2.82 (2.64 m 33/2).
Weight: 76-78 t.	**Wheel Diameter:** 1092 mm.
Design Speed: 85 mph.	**Maximum Speed:** 85 mph.
Fuel Capacity: 3410 litres.	**Route Availability:** 6.

Train Supply: Electric, index 48 (750 V DC only).
Total: 5.

Non-standard numbering: 33012 Carries original number D6515.

Class 33/0. Standard Design.

33012	**G**	71	MBDL	SW	Lt Jenny Lewis RN
33025	**WC**	WC	AWCA	CS	
33029	**WC**	WC	AWCA	CS	
33030	**DR**	WC	AWCX	CS (S)	

Class 33/2. Built to former Loading Gauge of Tonbridge–Battle Line.
Equipped with slow speed control.

33207	**WC**	WC	AWCA	CS	Jim Martin

CLASS 37   ENGLISH ELECTRIC   Co-Co

Built: 1960–66 by English Electric at Vulcan Foundry, Newton-le-Willows or by Robert Stephenson & Hawthorns at Darlington.
Engine: English Electric 12CSVT of 1300 kW (1750 hp) at 850 rpm.
Main Generator: English Electric 822/10G.
Traction Motors: English Electric 538/A.
Maximum Tractive Effort: 247 kN (55500 lbf).
Continuous Tractive Effort: 156 kN (35000 lbf) at 13.6 mph.
Power at Rail: 932 kW (1250 hp).   **Train Brakes:** Air & vacuum.
Brake Force: 50 t.   **Dimensions:** 18.75 x 2.74 m.
Weight: 102.8–108.4 t.   **Wheel Diameter:** 1092 mm.
Design Speed: 90 mph.   **Maximum Speed:** 80 mph.
Fuel Capacity: 4046 (+ 7683) litres.   **Route Availability:** 5 (§ 6).
Train Supply: Not equipped.   **Total:** 67.

Non-standard numbering:

37057   Also carries original number D6757.
37424   Also carries the number 37558.
37703   Carries the number 37067.
37905   Also carries original number D6838.

Class 37/0. Standard Design.

37025	**BL**	37	COTS	BH	Inverness TMD
37038 a	**DI**	DR	XHNC	KM	
37057	**G**	CS	COTS	BH	
37059 ar+	**DI**	DR	XHNC	KM	
37069 ar+	**DI**	DR	XHNC	KM	
37099	**CS**	CS	COTS	BH	MERL EVANS 1947–2016
37116 +	**CS**	CS	COTS	BH	
37146	**CE**	CE	COLS	Studley (S)	
37165 a+	**CE**	WC	AWCX	CS (S)	
37175 a	**CS**	CS	COTS	BH	
37188	**F**	CS	COLS	BH (S)	
37198 +	**Y**	NR	MBDL	ZA (S)	
37207	**B**	CS	COLS	BH (S)	
37218 ar+	**DI**	DR	XHNC	KM	
37219	**CS**	CS	COTS	BH	Jonty Jarvis 8-12-1998 to 18-3-2005
37254	**CS**	CS	COTS	BH	Cardiff Canton
37259 ar	**DS**	DR	XHNC	KM	

Class 37/4. Refurbished with electric train supply equipment. Main generator replaced by alternator. Regeared (CP7) bogies. Details as Class 37/0 except:
Main Alternator: Brush BA1005A.   **Power At Rail:** 935 kW (1254 hp).
Traction Motors: English Electric 538/5A.
Maximum Tractive Effort: 256 kN (57440 lbf).
Continuous Tractive Effort: 184 kN (41250 lbf) at 11.4 mph.
Weight: 107 t.   **Design Speed:** 80 mph.
Fuel Capacity: 7683 litres.
Train Supply: Electric, index 30.

37401 ar	**BL**	DR	XHCC	KM	Mary Queen of Scots

37402 a	**BL**	DR	XHSS	KM (S)	Stephen Middlemore 23.12.1954–8.6.2013
37403	**BL**	SP	XHCC	KM	Isle of Mull
37405 ar	**DS**	DR	XHAC	KM	
37407	**BL**	DR	XHAC	KM	
37409 ar	**BL**	DR	XHAC	KM	Lord Hinton
37418	**BL**	HN	MBDL	BH (S)	
37419 ar	**DS**	DR	XHAC	KM	Carl Haviland 1954–2012
37421	**CS**	CS	COTS	BH	
37422 ar	**DR**	DR	XHAC	KM	
37423 ar	**DR**	DR	XHAC	KM	Spirit of the Lakes
37424	**BL**	DR	XHCC	KM	Avro Vulcan XH558
37425 ar	**DS**	DR	XHCC	KM	Sir Robert McAlpine/Concrete Bob

Class 37/5. Refurbished without train supply equipment. Main generator replaced by alternator. Regeared (CP7) bogies. Details as Class 37/4 except:
Power At Rail: 932 kW (1250 hp).
Maximum Tractive Effort: 248 kN (55590 lbf).
Weight: 106.1–110.0 t.
Train Supply: Not equipped.

37503 r§	**E**	EP	EPUK	LR (S)	
37510 a	**DS**	EP	SROG	LR (S)	
37516 s	**WC**	WC	AWCA	CS	Loch Laidon
37517 as	**LH**	WC	AWCX	CS (S)	
37518 ar	**WC**	WC	AWCA	CS	
37521	**CS**	HN	COTS	BH	

Class 37/6. Originally refurbished for Nightstar services. Main generator replaced by alternator. UIC jumpers. Details as Class 37/5 except:
Maximum Speed: 90 mph.   **Train Brake:** Air.
Train Supply: Not equipped, but electric through wired.

37601 ad	**EX**	EP	GROG	LR	Perseus
37602 ar	**DS**	DR	XHNC	KM	
37603 a	**DS**	DR	XHSS	LW (S)	
37604 a	**DS**	DR	XHSS	LW (S)	
37605 ar	**DS**	DR	XHNC	KM	
37606 a	**DS**	DR	XHNC	KM	
37607 ar	**DR**	HN	COTS	BH	
37608 ard	**EX**	EP	GROG	LR	Andromeda
37609 a	**DI**	DR	XHSS	LW (S)	
37610 ar	**BL**	HN	COTS	BH	
37611 ad	**EX**	EP	GROG	LR	Pegasus
37612 a	**DR**	HN	COTS	BH	

Class 37/5 continued.

37667 ars	**DS**	LD	MBDL	CL (S)	
37668 e	**WC**	WC	AWCA	CS	
37669 e	**WC**	WC	AWCA	CS	
37676 a	**WC**	WC	AWCA	CS (S)	Loch Rannoch
37685 a	**WC**	WC	AWCA	CS	Loch Arkaig

Class 37/7. Refurbished locomotives. Main generator replaced by alternator. Regeared (CP7) bogies. Ballast weights added. Details as Class 37/5 except:
Main Alternator: GEC G564AZ (37800) Brush BA1005A (others).
Maximum Tractive Effort: 276 kN (62000 lbf).
Weight: 120 t. **Route Availability:** 7.

37703	**DR**	DR	XHSS	BO	
37706	**WC**	WC	AWCA	CS	
37710	**LH**	WC	AWCX	CS (S)	
37712 a	**WC**	WC	AWCX	CS (S)	
37716	**DI**	DR	XHNC	KM	
37800 d	**EX**	EP	GROG	LR	Cassiopeia
37884 d	**EX**	EP	GROG	LR	Cerpheus

Class 37/9. Refurbished locomotives. New power unit. Main generator replaced by alternator. Ballast weights added. Details as Class 37/4 except:
Engine: * Mirrlees 6MB275T of 1340 kW (1800 hp) or † Ruston 6RK270T of 1340 kW (1800 hp) at 900 rpm.
Main Alternator: Brush BA15005A.
Maximum Tractive Effort: 279 kN (62680 lbf).
Weight: 120 t. **Route Availability:** 7.
Train Supply: Not equipped.

37901 *	**EX**	90	COLS	LR	Mirrlees Pioneer
37905 †	**G**	UR	UKRM	LR (S)	
37906 †	**FO**	UR	UKRM	LR (S)	

Class 97/3. Class 37s refurbished for use on the Cambrian Lines which are signalled by ERTMS. Details as Class 37/0.

97301	(37100) e	**Y**	NR	QETS	ZA	
97302	(37170) e	**Y**	NR	QETS	ZA	
97303	(37178) e	**Y**	NR	QETS	ZA	
97304	(37217) e	**Y**	NR	QETS	ZA	John Tiley

CLASS 40 ENGLISH ELECTRIC 1Co-Co1

Built: 1961 by English Electric at Vulcan Foundry, Newton-le-Willows.
Engine: English Electric 16SVT Mk2 of 1492 kW (2000 hp) at 850 rpm.
Main Generator: English Electric 822/4C.
Traction Motors: English Electric 526/5D or EE526/7D.
Maximum Tractive Effort: 231 kN (52000 lbf).
Continuous Tractive Effort: 137 kN (30900 lbf) at 18.8 mph.

Power at Rail: 1160 kW (1550 hp).	**Train Brakes:** Air & vacuum.
Brake Force: 51 t.	**Dimensions:** 21.18 x 2.78 m.
Weight: 132 t.	**Wheel Diameter:** 914/1143 mm.
Design Speed: 90 mph.	**Maximum Speed:** 90 mph.
Fuel Capacity: 3250 litres.	**Route Availability:** 6.
Train Supply: Steam heating.	**Total:** 2.

40013 Carries original number D213.
40145 Carries original number 345.

40013	**G**	ST	MBDL	CL	Andania
40145	**B**	40	CFSL	BQ	

CLASS 43   BREL/PAXMAN   Bo-Bo

Built: 1975–82 by BREL at Crewe Works.
Engine: MTU 16V4000R41R of 1680kW (2250 hp) at 1500 rpm.
(* Paxman 12VP185 of 1680 kW (2250 hp) at 1500 rpm.)
Main Alternator: Brush BA1001B.
Traction Motors: Brush TMH68–46 or GEC G417AZ (43124–152); frame mounted.
Maximum Tractive Effort: 80 kN (17980 lbf).
Continuous Tractive Effort: 46 kN (10340 lbf) at 64.5 mph.
Power at Rail: 1320 kW (1770 hp).   **Train Brakes:** Air.
Brake Force: 35 t.   **Dimensions:** 17.79 x 2.74 m.
Weight: 70.25–75.0 t.   **Wheel Diameter:** 1020 mm.
Design Speed: 125 mph.   **Maximum Speed:** 125 mph.
Fuel Capacity: 4500 litres.   **Route Availability:** 5.
Train Supply: Three-phase electric.   **Total:** 194.

† Buffer fitted.
§ Modified Great Western Railway power cars that can operate with the power door fitted short sets.

43013, 43014 & 43062 are fitted with measuring apparatus & front-end cameras.

Power cars 43002, 43013, 43048, 43321 and 43423 carry small commemorative plates to celebrate 40 years of the HST, reading "40 YEARS 1976–2016".

Non-standard and advertising liveries:

43002   Original HST BR blue & yellow.
43027   90 Glorious Years (blue).
43172   We Shall Remember Them.
43238   National Railway Museum 40 Years.

43002	**0**	A	EFPC	LA	Sir Kenneth Grange
43003	**FB**	A	HAPC	HA	
43004 §	**FB**	A	EFPC	LA	
43005	**GW**	A	EFPC	LA	
43009	**FB**	A	EFPC	LA	
43010	**FB**	A	EFPC	LA	
43012	**SI**	A	HAPC	HA	
43013 †	**Y**	P	QCAR	EC	Mark Carne CBE
43014 †	**Y**	P	QCAR	EC	The Railway Observer
43015	**FB**	A	EFPC	LA	
43016 §	**GW**	A	EFPC	LA	
43017	**FB**	A	EFPC	LA	Hannahs discoverhannahs.org
43018	**FB**	A	EFPC	LA	
43020	**FB**	A	EFPC	LA	MTU Power. Passion. Partnership
43021	**FB**	A	HAPC	HA	
43022	**FB**	A	EFPC	LA	The Duke of Edinburgh's Award Diamond Anniversary 1956–2016
43023	**FB**	A	EFPC	LA	SQN LDR HAROLD STARR ONE OF THE FEW
43024	**FB**	A	EFPC	LA	Great Western Society 1961–2011 Didcot Railway Centre

43025	**FB**	A	EFPC	LA	IRO The Institution of Railway Operators 2000–2010 TEN YEARS PROMOTING OPERATIONAL EXCELLENCE
43026	**SI**	A	HAPC	EP (S)	
43027	**AL**	A	EFPC	LA	
43028	**FB**	A	HAPC	LB (S)	
43029	**FB**	A	EFPC	LA	
43030	**FB**	A	EFPC	LA	Christian Lewis Trust
43031	**FB**	A	HAPC	EP (S)	
43032	**SI**	A	HAPC	HA	
43033	**SI**	A	HAPC	HA	
43034	**FB**	A	EFPC	LA	
43035	**FB**	A	HAPC	HA	
43036	**SI**	A	HAPC	HA	
43037	**FB**	A	HAPC	HA	
43040 §	**GW**	A	EFPC	LA	
43041	**GW**	A	EFPC	LA	Meningitis Trust Support for Life
43042 §	**GW**	A	EFPC	LA	
43043 *	**ST**	P	EMPC	NL	
43044 *	**ST**	P	EMPC	NL	
43045 *	**ST**	P	EMPC	NL	
43046 *	**ST**	P	EMPC	NL	
43047 *	**ST**	P	EMPC	NL	
43048 *	**ST**	P	EMPC	NL	T.C.B. Miller MBE
43049 *	**ST**	P	EMPC	NL	Neville Hill
43050 *	**ST**	P	EMPC	NL	
43052 *	**ST**	P	EMPC	NL	
43053	**FB**	P	EFPC	LA	University of Worcester
43054 *	**ST**	P	EMPC	NL	
43055 *	**ST**	P	EMPC	NL	The Sheffield Star 125 Years
43056	**FB**	P	EFPC	LA	The Royal British Legion
43058 *	**ST**	P	EMPC	NL	
43059 *	**ST**	P	EMPC	NL	
43060 *	**ST**	P	EMPC	NL	
43061 *	**ST**	P	EMPC	NL	The Fearless Foxes
43062	**Y**	P	QCAR	EC	John Armitt
43063	**FB**	P	EFPC	LA	
43064 *	**ST**	P	EMPC	NL	
43066 *	**ST**	P	EMPC	NL	
43069	**FB**	P	EFPC	LA	
43070	**FB**	P	EFPC	LA	The Corps of Royal Electrical and Mechanical Engineers
43071	**FB**	P	EFPC	LA	
43073 *	**ST**	P	EMPC	NL	
43075 *	**ST**	P	EMPC	NL	
43076 *	**ST**	P	EMPC	NL	IN SUPPORT OF HELP for HEROES
43078	**FB**	P	EFPC	LA	
43079	**FB**	P	EFPC	LA	
43081 *	**ST**	P	EMPC	NL	
43082 *	**ST**	P	EMPC	NL	RAILWAY children – Fighting for street children

43083	*	**ST**	P	EMPC	NL	
43086		**FB**	P	EFPC	LA	
43087		**FB**	P	EFPC	LA	11 Explosive Ordnance Disposal
						Regiment Royal Logistic Corps
43088		**FB**	P	EFPC	LA	
43089	*	**ST**	P	EMPC	NL	
43091		**FB**	P	EFPC	LA	
43092	§	**GW**	FG	EFPC	LA	
43093	§	**GW**	FG	EFPC	LA	Old Oak Common HST Depot
						1976–2018
43094		**FB**	FG	EFPC	LA	
43097		**FB**	FG	EFPC	LA	Environment Agency
43098	§	**GW**	FG	EFPC	LA	
43122		**FB**	FG	EFPC	LA	
43124		**FB**	A	HAPC	HA	
43125		**SI**	A	HAPC	HA	
43126		**FB**	A	HAPC	HA	
43127		**FB**	A	HAPC	HA	
43128		**SI**	A	HAPC	EP (S)	
43129		**FB**	A	HAPC	EP (S)	
43130		**FB**	A	HAPC	LB (S)	
43131		**FB**	A	EFPC	LA	
43132		**FB**	A	HAPC	HA	Aberdeen Station 150th Anniversary
43133		**FB**	A	HAPC	HA	
43134		**SI**	A	HAPC	HA	
43135		**FB**	A	HAPC	HA	
43136		**FB**	A	HAPC	HA	
43137		**FB**	A	EFPC	LA	Newton Abbot 150
43138		**FB**	A	HAPC	EP (S)	
43139		**FB**	A	HAPC	LB (S)	
43140		**SI**	A	HAPC	HA	
43141		**SI**	A	EFPC	HA	
43142		**FB**	A	HAPC	HA	
43143		**SI**	A	HAPC	HA	
43144		**FB**	A	EFPC	LA	
43145		**FB**	A	HAPC	HA	
43146		**SI**	A	HAPC	HA	
43147		**FB**	A	EFPC	LA	Royal Marines
						Celebrating 350 Years
43148		**SI**	A	HAPC	HA	
43149		**SI**	A	HAPC	LA (S)	
43150		**FB**	A	HAPC	LB (S)	
43151		**FB**	A	EFPC	LA (S)	
43152		**FB**	A	EFPC	LB (S)	
43153	§	**GW**	FG	EFPC	LA	
43154		**FB**	FG	HAPC	LB (S)	
43155		**FB**	FG	EFPC	LA	The Red Arrows
						50 Seasons of Excellence
43156		**FB**	P	EFPC	LA	Dartington International Summer School
43158		**FB**	FG	EFPC	LA	
43159		**FB**	P	EFPC	LA	

43160	**FB**	P	EFPC	LA	Sir Moir Lockhead OBE
43161	**FB**	P	EFPC	LA	
43162	**FB**	P	EFPC	LA	Exeter Panel Signalbox 21st Anniversary 2009
43163	**SI**	A	HAPC	HA	
43164	**FB**	A	HAPC	LB (S)	
43165	**FB**	A	EFPC	LA	Prince Michael of Kent
43168	**SI**	A	HAPC	HA	
43169	**SI**	A	HAPC	HA	
43170 §	**GW**	A	EFPC	LA	
43171	**FB**	A	EFPC	LA	
43172	**AL**	A	EFPC	LA	Harry Patch – The last survivor of the trenches
43174	**FB**	A	EFPC	LA	
43175	**FB**	A	HAPC	HA	
43176	**FB**	A	HAPC	LB (S)	
43177	**FB**	A	HAPC	LB (S)	
43179	**FB**	A	HAPC	HA	
43180	**FB**	P	EFPC	LA	
43181	**FB**	A	EFPC	LA	
43182	**FB**	A	HAPC	EP (S)	
43183	**SI**	A	EFPC	HA	
43185	**IC**	A	EFPC	LA	Great Western
43186	**FB**	A	EFPC	LA	
43187 §	**GW**	A	EFPC	LA	
43188	**GW**	A	EFPC	LA	
43189 §	**GW**	A	EFPC	LA	
43190	**FB**	A	EFPC	LA	
43191	**FB**	A	EFPC	LA	
43192	**FB**	A	EFPC	LA	
43193	**FB**	P	EFPC	LA	
43194	**GW**	FG	EFPC	LA	
43195	**FB**	P	EFPC	LA (S)	
43196	**FB**	P	EFPC	LA	
43197	**FB**	P	EFPC	LA	
43198 §	**GW**	FG	EFPC	LA	Oxfordshire 2007

Class 43/2. Rebuilt LNER, CrossCountry and East Midlands Trains (former Grand Central) power cars. Power cars have been renumbered by adding 200 to their original number or 400 to their original number (EMT), except 43123 which became 43423.

43206	(43006)	**VE**	A	IECP	EC	
43207	(43007)	**XC**	A	EHPC	EC	
43208	(43008)	**VE**	A	IECP	EC	Lincolnshire Echo
43238	(43038)	**AL**	A	IECP	EC	National Railway Museum 40 Years 1975–2015
43239	(43039)	**VE**	A	IECP	EC	
43251	(43051)	**VE**	P	IECP	EC	
43257	(43057)	**VE**	P	IECP	EC	Bounds Green
43272	(43072)	**VE**	P	IECP	EC	

43274	(43074)	**VE**	P	IECP	EC	Spirit of Sunderland
43277	(43077)	**VE**	P	IECP	EC	
43285	(43085)	**XC**	P	EHPC	EC	
43290	(43090)	**VE**	P	IECP	EC	mtu fascination of power
43295	(43095)	**VE**	A	IECP	EC	
43296	(43096)	**VE**	A	IECP	EC	
43299	(43099)	**VE**	P	IECP	EC	
43300	(43100)	**VE**	P	IECP	EC	Craigentinny 100 YEARS 1914–2014
43301	(43101)	**XC**	P	EHPC	EC	
43302	(43102)	**VE**	P	IECP	EC	World Speed Record – HST
43303	(43103)	**XC**	P	EHPC	EC	
43304	(43104)	**XC**	A	EHPC	EC	
43305	(43105)	**VE**	A	IECP	EC	
43306	(43106)	**VE**	A	IECP	EC	
43307	(43107)	**VE**	A	IECP	EC	
43308	(43108)	**VE**	A	IECP	EC	HIGHLAND CHIEFTAIN
43309	(43109)	**VE**	A	IECP	EC	
43310	(43110)	**VE**	A	IECP	EC	
43311	(43111)	**VE**	A	IECP	EC	
43312	(43112)	**VE**	A	IECP	EC	
43313	(43113)	**VE**	A	IECP	EC	
43314	(43114)	**VE**	A	IECP	EC	
43315	(43115)	**VE**	A	IECP	EC	
43316	(43116)	**VE**	A	IECP	EC	
43317	(43117)	**VE**	A	IECP	EC	
43318	(43118)	**VE**	A	IECP	EC	
43319	(43119)	**VE**	A	IECP	EC	
43320	(43120)	**VE**	A	IECP	EC	
43321	(43121)	**XC**	P	EHPC	EC	
43357	(43157)	**XC**	P	EHPC	EC	
43366	(43166)	**XC**	A	EHPC	EC	
43367	(43167)	**VE**	A	IECP	EC	DELTIC 50 1955–2005
43378	(43178)	**XC**	A	EHPC	EC	
43384	(43184)	**XC**	A	EHPC	EC	
43423	(43123) †	**EA**	A	EMPC	DY	'VALENTA' 1972–2010
43465	(43065) †	**EA**	A	EMPC	DY	
43467	(43067) †	**EA**	A	EMPC	DY	Nottinghamshire Fire and Rescue Service/ British Transport Police Nottingham
43468	(43068) †	**EA**	A	EMPC	DY	
43480	(43080) †	**EA**	A	EMPC	DY	
43484	(43084) †	**EA**	A	EMPC	DY	

CLASS 47   BR/BRUSH/SULZER   Co-Co

Built: 1963–67 by Brush Traction, at Loughborough or by BR at Crewe Works.
Engine: Sulzer 12LDA28C of 1920 kW (2580 hp) at 750 rpm.
Main Generator: Brush TG160-60 Mk4 or TM172-50 Mk1.
Traction Motors: Brush TM64-68 Mk1 or Mk1A.
Maximum Tractive Effort: 267 kN (60000 lbf).
Continuous Tractive Effort: 133 kN (30000 lbf) at 26 mph.
Power at Rail: 1550 kW (2080 hp).   **Train Brakes:** Air.
Brake Force: 61 t.   **Dimensions:** 19.38 x 2.79 m.
Weight: 111.5–120.6 t.   **Wheel Diameter:** 1143 mm.
Design Speed: 95 mph.   **Maximum Speed:** 95 mph.
Fuel Capacity: 3273 (+ 5887).   **Route Availability:** 6 or 7.
Train Supply: Not equipped.   **Total:** 47.

Class 47s exported for use abroad are listed in section 5 of this book.

Non-standard liveries/numbering:

47270   Also carries original number 1971.
47501   Carries original number D1944.
47773   Also carries original number D1755.
47798   Royal Train claret with Rail Express Systems markings.
47805   Carries original number D1935.
47810   Carries original number D1924.
47830   Also carries original number D1645.
47853   Carries original number 1733.

Class 47/0. Standard Design. Built with train air and vacuum brakes.

47194 +	**F**	WC	AWCX	CS (S)	
47237 x+	**WC**	WC	AWCA	CS	
47245 x+	**WC**	WC	AWCA	CS	
47270 +	**B**	WC	AWCA	CS	SWIFT

Class 47/3. Built with train air and vacuum brakes. Details as Class 47/0 except: **Weight:** 113.7 t.

47355 a+	**K**	WC	AWCX	CS (S)	
47368	**F**	WC	AWCX	CS (S)	

Class 47/4. Electric Train Supply equipment.
Details as Class 47/0 except:

Weight: 120.4–125.1 t.   **Fuel Capacity:** 3273 (+ 5537) litres.
Train Supply: Electric, index 66.   **Route Availability:** 7.

47492 x	**RX**	WC	AWCX	CS (S)	
47500 x	**WC**	WC	AWCX	CS (S)	
47501 x+	**GG**	LD	MBDL	CL	CRAFTSMAN
47526 x	**BL**	WC	AWCX	CS (S)	
47580 x	**BL**	47	MBDL	TM	County of Essex

Class 47/7. Previously fitted with an older form of TDM.
Details as Class 47/4 except:

Weight: 118.7 t.   **Fuel Capacity:** 5887 litres.
Maximum Speed: 100 mph.

| 47703 | **FR** | HN | HNRL | ZB |
| 47714 | **AR** | HN | HNRL | Old Dalby |

Class 47/7. Former Railnet dedicated locomotives.
Details as Class 47/0 except:

Fuel Capacity: 5887 litres.

47727	**CA**	GB	GBDF	ZG	Edinburgh Castle/
					Caisteal Dhùn Èideann
47739	**CS**	GB	GBDF	ZG	
47746 x	**WC**	WC	AWCA	CS	Chris Fudge 29.7.70 – 22.6.10
47749	**CS**	GB	GBDF	ZG	CITY OF TRURO
47760 x	**WC**	WC	AWCA	CS	
47768	**RX**	WC	AWCX	CS (S)	
47769	**V**	HN	HNRS	BH (S)	Resolve
47772 x	**WC**	WC	AWCA	CS	Carnforth TMD
47773 x	**GG**	70	MBDL	TM	
47776 x	**RX**	WC	AWCX	CS (S)	
47786	**WC**	WC	AWCA	CS	Roy Castle OBE
47787	**WC**	WC	AWCX	CS (S)	
47790	**VN**	LD	MBDL	CL	

Class 47/4 continued. Route Availability: 6.

47798 x	**O**	NM	MBDL	YK	Prince William
47802 +	**WC**	WC	AWCA	CS	
47804 +	**WC**	WC	AWCA	CS	
47805 +	**GG**	LD	MBDL	CL	Roger Hosking MA 1925–2013
47810 +	**GG**	LD	MBDL	CL	Crewe Diesel Depot
47811 +	**GL**	LD	DHLT	CL (S)	
47812 +	**RB**	RO	GROG	LR	
47813 +	**RO**	RO	SROG	LR	
47815 +	**RB**	RO	GROG	LR	
47816 +	**GL**	LD	DHLT	CL (S)	
47818 +	**DS**	AF	MBDL	ZG (S)	
47826 +	**WC**	WC	AWCA	CS	
47830 +	**GG**	FL	DFLH	CB	BEECHING'S LEGACY
47832 +	**WC**	WC	AWCA	CS	
47841 +	**DS**	LD	MBDL	CL (S)	
47843 +	**RB**	RO	SROG	LR (S)	
47847 +	**BL**	RO	SROG	LR (S)	
47848 +	**RB**	RO	SROG	LR	
47851 +	**WC**	WC	AWCA	CS	
47853 +	**B**	LD	MBDL	CL	
47854 +	**WC**	WC	AWCA	CS	Diamond Jubilee

CLASS 50   ENGLISH ELECTRIC   Co-Co

Built: 1967–68 by English Electric at Vulcan Foundry, Newton-le-Willows.
Engine: English Electric 16CVST of 2010 kW (2700 hp) at 850 rpm.
Main Generator: English Electric 840/4B.
Traction Motors: English Electric 538/5A.
Maximum Tractive Effort: 216 kN (48500 lbf).
Continuous Tractive Effort: 147 kN (33000 lbf) at 23.5 mph.

Power at Rail: 1540 kW (2070 hp).	**Train Brakes:** Air & vacuum.
Brake Force: 59 t.	**Dimensions:** 20.88 x 2.78 m.
Weight: 116.9 t.	**Wheel Diameter:** 1092 mm.
Design Speed: 105 mph.	**Maximum Speed:** 90 mph.
Fuel Capacity: 4796 litres.	**Route Availability:** 6.
Train Supply: Electric, index 61.	**Total:** 6.

Non-standard numbering:

50007 Also carries original number D407.
50050 Also carries original number D400.

50007	B	50	CFOL	KR	Hercules
50008	B	HT	HTLX	LR	Thunderer
50017	N	NB	MBDL	NM	Royal Oak
50044	B	50	CFOL	KR	Exeter
50049	BL	50	CFOL	KR	Defiance
50050	B	NB	MBDL	NM	Fearless

CLASS 52   BR/MAYBACH   C-C

Built: 1961–64 by BR at Swindon Works.
Engine: Two Maybach MD655 of 1007 kW (1350 hp) each at 1500 rpm.
Transmission: Hydraulic. Voith L630rV.
Maximum Tractive Effort: 297 kN (66700 lbf).
Continuous Tractive Effort: 201 kN (45200 lbf) at 14.5 mph.

Power at Rail: 1490 kW (2000 hp).	**Train Brakes:** Air & vacuum.
Brake Force: 83 t.	**Dimensions:** 20.70 m x 2.78 m.
Weight: 110 t.	**Wheel Diameter:** 1092 mm.
Design Speed: 90 mph.	**Maximum Speed:** 90 mph.
Fuel Capacity: 3900 litres.	**Route Availability:** 6.
Train Supply: Steam heating.	**Total:** 1.

Never allocated a number in the 1972 number series.

D1015	M	DT	MBDL	KR	WESTERN CHAMPION

CLASS 55   ENGLISH ELECTRIC Co-Co

Built: 1961 by English Electric at Vulcan Foundry, Newton-le-Willows.
Engine: Two Napier-Deltic D18-25 of 1230 kW (1650 hp) each at 1500 rpm.
Main Generators: Two English Electric 829/1A.
Traction Motors: English Electric 538/A.
Maximum Tractive Effort: 222 kN (50000 lbf).
Continuous Tractive Effort: 136 kN (30500 lbf) at 32.5 mph.
Power at Rail: 1969 kW (2640 hp).   **Train Brakes:** Air & vacuum.
Brake Force: 51 t.   **Dimensions:** 21.18 x 2.68 m.
Weight: 100 t.   **Wheel Diameter:** 1092 mm.
Design Speed: 105 mph.   **Maximum Speed:** 100 mph.
Fuel Capacity: 3755 litres.   **Route Availability:** 5.
Train Supply: Electric, index 66. **Total:** 4.
Non-standard numbering:

55002		Carries orignal number D9002.		
55009		Carries orignal number D9009.		
55016		Carries orignal number D9016.		

55002	**GG**	NM	MBDL	YK	THE KING'S OWN YORKSHIRE LIGHT INFANTRY
55009	**B**	DP	MBDL	BH	ALYCIDON
55016	**GG**	LD	MBDL	CL (S)	GORDON HIGHLANDER
55022	**B**	LD	MBDL	CL	ROYAL SCOTS GREY

CLASS 56   BRUSH/BR/RUSTON Co-Co

Built: 1976–84 by Electroputere at Craiova, Romania (as sub-contractors for Brush) or BREL at Doncaster or Crewe Works.
Engine: Ruston Paxman 16RK3CT of 2460 kW (3250 hp) at 900 rpm.
Main Alternator: Brush BA1101A.
Traction Motors: Brush TM73-62.
Maximum Tractive Effort: 275 kN (61800 lbf).
Continuous Tractive Effort: 240 kN (53950 lbf) at 16.8 mph.
Power at Rail: 1790 kW (2400 hp).   **Train Brakes:** Air.
Brake Force: 60 t.   **Dimensions:** 19.36 x 2.79 m.
Weight: 126 t.   **Wheel Diameter:** 1143 mm.
Design Speed: 80 mph.   **Maximum Speed:** 80 mph.
Fuel Capacity: 5228 litres.   **Route Availability:** 7.
Train Supply: Not equipped.   **Total:** 32.

All equipped with Slow Speed Control.

Class 56s exported for use abroad are listed in section 5 of this book.

Non-standard liveries:

56009 All over blue.
56303 All over dark green.

56007	**B**	GB	UKRS	LR (S)
56009	**0**	GB	UKRS	LT (S)

56018	**FER**	GB	UKRS	CN (S)	
56031	**FER**	GB	GBGS	LT (S)	
56032	**FER**	GB	GBGS	LT (S)	
56037	**E**	GB	GBGS	LT (S)	
56038	**FER**	GB	UKRS	LR (S)	
56049	**CS**	CS	COFS	NM	Robin of Templecombe 1938–2013
56051	**CS**	CS	COLS	NM (S)	
56060	**FER**	GB	UKRS	LR (S)	
56065	**FER**	GB	UKRS	LR (S)	
56069	**FER**	GB	GBGS	LT (S)	
56077	**LH**	GB	UKRS	LR (S)	
56078	**CS**	CS	COFS	NM	
56081	**FO**	GB	UKRL	LR (S)	
56087	**CS**	CS	COFS	NM	
56090	**CS**	CS	COFS	NM	
56091	**FER**	DC	HTLX	LR (S)	
56094	**CS**	CS	COFS	NM	
56096	**CS**	CS	COFS	NM	
56098	**FO**	GB	UKRL	CN (S)	
56103	**DC**	DC	HTLX	LR	
56104	**FO**	GB	UKRL	CN (S)	
56105	**CS**	CS	COFS	NM	
56106	**FER**	GB	UKRS	LR (S)	
56113	**CS**	CS	COFS	NM	
56128	**F**	GB		LT (S)	
56301 (56045)		**FA**	56	UKRL	LR	
56302 (56124)		**CS**	CS	COFS	NM	PECO The Railway Modeller 2016 70 Years
56303 (56125)		**O**	GB	HTLX	LR (S)	
56311 (56057)		**DC**	GB	GBGS	LR (S)	
56312 (56003)		**DC**	GB	HTLX	LR (S)	

CLASS 57   BRUSH/GM   Co-Co

Built: 1964–65 by Brush Traction at Loughborough or BR at Crewe Works as Class 47. Rebuilt 1997–2004 by Brush Traction at Loughborough.
Engine: General Motors 12 645 E3 of 1860 kW (2500 hp) at 904 rpm.
Main Alternator: Brush BA1101D (recovered from Class 56).
Traction Motors: Brush TM64-68 Mark 1 or Mark 1A.
Maximum Tractive Effort: 244.5 kN (55000 lbf).
Continuous Tractive Effort: 140 kN (31500 lbf) at ?? mph.

Power at Rail: 1507 kW (2025 hp).	**Train Brakes:** Air.
Brake Force: 80 t.	**Dimensions:** 19.38 x 2.79 m.
Weight: 120.6 t.	**Wheel Diameter:** 1143 mm.
Design Speed: 75 mph.	**Maximum Speed:** 75 mph.
Fuel Capacity: 5550 litres.	**Route Availability:** 6
Train Supply: Not equipped.	**Total:** 33.

Non-standard livery: 57604 Original Great Western Railway green.

Class 57/0. No Train Supply Equipment. Rebuilt 1997–2000.

57001 (47356)	**WC**	WC	AWCA	CS (S)	
57002 (47322)	**DI**	DR	XHCK	KM	RAIL EXPRESS
57003 (47317)	**DI**	DR	XHCK	KM	
57004 (47347)	**DS**	DR	XHSS	LW (S)	
57005 (47350)	**AZ**	WC	AWCX	CS (S)	
57006 (47187)	**WC**	WC	AWCX	CS (S)	
57007 (47332)	**DI**	DR	XHCK	KM	John Scott 12.5.45–22.5.12
57008 (47060)	**DS**	DR	XHSS	LW (S)	
57009 (47079)	**DS**	DR	XHSS	LW (S)	
57010 (47231)	**DI**	DR	XHSS	LW (S)	
57011 (47329)	**DS**	DR	XHSS	LW (S)	
57012 (47204)	**DS**	DR	XHSS	LW (S)	

Class 57/3. Electric Train Supply Equipment. Former Virgin Trains locomotives fitted with retractable Dellner couplers. Rebuilt 2002–04. Details as Class 57/0 except:

Engine: General Motors 12645F3B of 2050 kW (2750 hp) at 954 rpm.
Main Alternator: Brush BA1101F (recovered from Class 56) or Brush BA1101G.
Fuel Capacity: 5887 litres.   **Train Supply:** Electric, index 100.
Design Speed: 95 mph.   **Maximum Speed:** 95 mph.
Brake Force: 60 t.   **Weight:** 117 t.

57301 (47845)	d	**DI**	P	XHAC	KM	Goliath
57302 (47827)	d	**DS**	DR	XHSS	ZG (S)	Chad Varah
57303 (47705)	d	**DI**	P	XHAC	KM	Pride of Carlisle
57304 (47807)	d	**DI**	DR	XHVT	KM	Pride of Cheshire
57305 (47822)	d	**VN**	P	GROG	LR	Northern Princess
57306 (47814)	d	**DI**	P	XHAC	KM	Her Majesty's Railway Inspectorate 175
57307 (47225)	d	**DI**	DR	XHVT	KM	LADY PENELOPE
57308 (47846)	d	**DI**	DR	XHVT	KM	Jamie Ferguson
57309 (47806)	d	**DI**	DR	XHVT	KM	Pride of Crewe
57310 (47831)	d	**DI**	P	XHSS	KM (S)	Pride of Cumbria
57311 (47817)	d	**DS**	DR	XHSS	LW (S)	Thunderbird
57312 (47330)	d	**VN**	P	GROG	LR	Solway Princess
57313 (47371)		**WC**	WC	AWCA	CS	
57314 (47372)		**WC**	WC	AWCA	CS	
57315 (47234)		**WC**	WC	AWCA	CS	
57316 (47290)		**WC**	WC	AWCA	CS	

Class 57/6. Electric Train Supply Equipment. Prototype ETS loco. Rebuilt 2001. Details as Class 57/0 except:

Main Alternator: Brush BA1101E.   **Fuel Capacity:** 3273 litres.
Train Supply: Electric, index 95.   **Weight:** 113t.
Design Speed: 95 mph.   **Maximum Speed:** 95 mph.
Brake Force: 60 t.

57601 (47825)	**PC**	WC	AWCA	CS	Windsor Castle

Class 57/6. Electric Train Supply Equipment. Great Western Railway locomotives. Rebuilt 2004. Details as Class 57/3.

57602 (47337)	**GW** P	EFOO	PZ	Restormel Castle
57603 (47349)	**GW** P	EFOO	PZ	Tintagel Castle
57604 (47209)	**0** P	EFOO	PZ	PENDENNIS CASTLE
57605 (47206)	**GW** P	EFOO	PZ	Totnes Castle

CLASS 59   GENERAL MOTORS   Co-Co

Built: 1985 (59001–004) or 1989 (59005) by General Motors, La Grange, Illinois, USA or 1990 (59101–104), 1994 (59201) and 1995 (59202–206) by General Motors, London, Ontario, Canada.
Engine: General Motors 16-645E3C two stroke of 2460 kW (3300 hp) at 904 rpm.
Main Alternator: General Motors AR11 MLD-D14A.
Traction Motors: General Motors D77B.
Maximum Tractive Effort: 506 kN (113550 lbf).
Continuous Tractive Effort: 291 kN (65300 lbf) at 14.3 mph.
Power at Rail: 1889 kW (2533 hp).   **Train Brakes:** Air.
Brake Force: 69 t.   **Dimensions:** 21.35 x 2.65 m.
Weight: 121 t.   **Wheel Diameter:** 1067 mm.
Design Speed: 60 (* 75) mph.   **Maximum Speed:** 60 (* 75) mph.
Fuel Capacity: 4546 litres.   **Route Availability:** 7.
Train Supply: Not equipped.   **Total:** 15.

Class 59/0. Owned by Aggregate Industries and GB Railfreight.

59001	**AI**	AI	XYPO	MD	YEOMAN ENDEAVOUR
59002	**AI**	AI	XYPO	MD	ALAN J DAY
59003	**GB**	GB	GBYH	RR	YEOMAN HIGHLANDER
59004	**AI**	AI	XYPO	MD	PAUL A HAMMOND
59005	**AI**	AI	XYPO	MD	KENNETH J PAINTER

Class 59/1. Owned by Hanson UK.

59101	**HA**	HA	XYPA	MD	Village of Whatley
59102	**HA**	HA	XYPA	MD	Village of Chantry
59103	**HA**	HA	XYPA	MD	Village of Mells
59104	**HA**	HA	XYPA	MD	Village of Great Elm

Class 59/2. Owned by DB Cargo.

59201 *	**DB**	DB	WDAM	MD	
59202 *	**DB**	DB	WDAM	MD	Alan Meddows Taylor MD Mendip Rail Limited
59203 *	**DB**	DB	WDAM	MD	
59204 *	**DB**	DB	WDAM	MD	
59205 *b	**DB**	DB	WDAM	MD	
59206 *b	**DB**	DB	WDAM	MD	John F. Yeoman Rail Pioneer

CLASS 60   BRUSH/MIRRLEES   Co-Co

Built: 1989–93 by Brush Traction at Loughborough.
Engine: Mirrlees 8MB275T of 2310 kW (3100 hp) at 1000 rpm.
Main Alternator: Brush BA1006A.
Traction Motors: Brush TM2161A.
Maximum Tractive Effort: 500 kN (106500 lbf).
Continuous Tractive Effort: 336 kN (71570 lbf) at 17.4 mph.
Power at Rail: 1800 kW (2415 hp).   **Train Brakes:** Air.
Brake Force: 74 t (+ 62 t).   **Dimensions:** 21.34 x 2.64 m.
Weight: 129 t (+ 131 t).   **Wheel Diameter:** 1118 mm.
Design Speed: 62 mph.   **Maximum Speed:** 60 mph.
Fuel Capacity: 4546 (+ 5225) litres. **Route Availability:** 8.
Train Supply: Not equipped.   **Total:** 100.

All equipped with Slow Speed Control.

* Refurbished locomotives.

60034, 60064, 60070, 60072, 60073, 60077, 60084 and 60090 carry their names on one side only.

60500 originally carried the number 60016.

Non-standard and Advertising liveries:

60066 Powering Drax (silver).
60081 Original Great Western Railway green.
60099 Tata Steel (silver).

60001 *	**DB**	DB	WCAT	TO	
60002 +*	**CS**	BN	GBTG	RR	
60003 +	**E**	DB	WQDA	TO (S)	FREIGHT TRANSPORT ASSOCIATION
60004 +	**E**	DB	WQDA	TO (S)	
60005 +	**E**	DB	WQDA	TO (S)	
60006	**CU**	DB	WQDA	TO (S)	
60007 +*	**DB**	DB	WCBT	TO	The Spirit of Tom Kendell
60008	**E**	DB	WQDA	TO (S)	Sir William McAlpine
60009 +	**E**	DB	WQBA	TO (S)	
60010 +*	**DB**	DB	WCBT	TO	
60011	**DB**	DB	WCAT	TO	
60012 +	**E**	DB	WQBA	TO (S)	
60013	**EG**	DB	WQDA	TO (S)	Robert Boyle
60014	**EG**	DB	WQDA	TO (S)	
60015 +*	**DB**	DB	WCBT	TO	
60017 +*	**DB**	DB	WCBT	TO	
60018	**E**	DB	WQDA	TO (S)	
60019 *	**DB**	DB	WCAT	TO	Port of Grimsby & Immingham
60020 +*	**DB**	DB	WCBT	TO	The Willows
60021 +*	**CS**	BN	GBTG	RR	
60022 +	**E**	DB	WQDA	TO (S)	
60023 +	**E**	DB	WQDA	TO (S)	
60024 *	**DB**	DB	WQAB	TO (S)	Clitheroe Castle
60025 +	**E**	DB	WQDA	TO (S)	

60026	+* CS	BN	GBTG	RR	
60027	+ E	DB	WQDA	TO (S)	
60028	+ EG	DB	WQCA	CE (S)	
60029	E	DB	WQCA	CE (S)	
60030	+ E	DB	WQDA	TO (S)	
60031	E	DB	WQDA	TO (S)	
60032	F	DB	WQDA	TO (S)	
60033	+ CU	DB	WQCA	TO (S)	Tees Steel Express
60034	EG	DB	WQBA	TO (S)	Carnedd Llewelyn
60035	E	DB	WQBA	TO (S)	
60036	E	DB	WQBA	TO (S)	GEFCO
60037	+ E	DB	WQDA	TO (S)	
60038	+ E	DB	WQCA	CE (S)	
60039	* DB	DB	WCAT	TO	Dove Holes
60040	* DB	DB	WCAT	TO	The Territorial Army Centenary
60041	+ E	DB	WQCA	TO (S)	
60042	E	DB	WQDA	TO (S)	
60043	E	DB	WQBA	TO (S)	
60044	* DB	DB	WCAT	TO	Dowlow
60045	E	DB	WQBA	TO (S)	The Permanent Way Institution
60046	+ EG	DB	WQCA	CE (S)	
60047	* CS	BN	GBTG	RR	
60048	E	DB	WQCA	TO (S)	
60049	E	DB	WQBA	TO (S)	
60050	E	DB	WQDA	TO (S)	
60051	+ E	DB	WQDA	TO (S)	
60052	+ E	DB	WQDA	TO (S)	Glofa Twr – The last deep mine in Wales – Tower Colliery
60053	E	DB	WQBA	TO (S)	
60054	+* DB	DB	WCBT	TO	
60055	+ EG	DB	WQCA	CE (S)	
60056	+* CS	BN	GBTG	RR	
60057	EG	DB	WQBA	TO (S)	Adam Smith
60058	+ E	DB	WQBA	TO (S)	
60059	+* DB	DB	WCBT	TO	Swinden Dalesman
60060	EG	DB	WQBA	TO (S)	
60061	F	DB	WQCA	TO (S)	
60062	* DB	DB	WCAT	TO	Stainless Pioneer
60063	* DB	DB	WCAT	TO	
60064	+ EG	DB	WQBA	TO (S)	Back Tor
60065	E	DB	WCAT	TO	Spirit of JAGUAR
60066	* AL	DB	WCAT	TO	
60067	EG	DB	WQBA	TO (S)	
60068	EG	DB	WQBA	TO (S)	
60069	E	DB	WQBA	TO (S)	Slioch
60070	+ F	DB	WQBA	TO (S)	John Loudon McAdam
60071	+ E	DB	WQBA	TO (S)	Ribblehead Viaduct
60072	EG	DB	WQBA	TO (S)	Cairn Toul
60073	EG	DB	WQBA	TO (S)	Cairn Gorm
60074	* DB	DB	WQAA	TO (S)	
60075	E	DB	WQBA	TO (S)	

60076	*	CS	GB	GBTG	RR	
60077	+	EG	DB	WQBA	TO (S)	Canisp
60078		ML	DB	WQBA	TO (S)	
60079	*	DB	DB	WQAB	TO (S)	
60080	+	E	DB	WQBA	TO (S)	
60081	+	O	DB	WQBA	TO (S)	
60082		EG	DB	WQBA	CE (S)	
60083		E	DB	WQBA	TO (S)	
60084		EG	DB	WQBA	TO (S)	Cross Fell
60085	*	CS	BN	GBTG	RR	
60086		EG	DB	WQBA	TO (S)	
60087	*	CS	BN	GBTG	RR	
60088		F	DB	WQBA	TO (S)	
60089	+	E	DB	WQBA	TO (S)	
60090	+	EG	DB	WQBA	TO (S)	Quinag
60091	+*	DB	DB	WCBT	TO	Barry Needham
60092	+*	DB	DB	WQAA	TO	
60093		E	DB	WQBA	TO (S)	
60094		E	DB	WQBA	TO (S)	Rugby Flyer
60095	*	GB	BN	GBTG	RR	
60096	+*	CS	BN	GBTG	RR	
60097	+	E	DB	WQBA	TO (S)	
60098	+	E	DB	WQBA	TO (S)	
60099		AL	DB	WQBA	TO (S)	
60100	*	DB	DB	WCAT	TO	Midland Railway-Butterley
60500		E	DB	WQBA	TO (S)	

CLASS 66   GENERAL MOTORS/EMD   Co-Co

Built: 1998–2008 by General Motors/EMD, London, Ontario, Canada (Model JT42CWR (low emission locomotives Model JT42CWRM)) or 2013–16 by EMD/Progress Rail, Muncie, Indiana (66752–779).
Engine: General Motors 12N-710G3B-EC two stroke of 2385 kW (3200 hp) at 904 rpm.
Main Alternator: General Motors AR8/CA6.
Traction Motors: General Motors D43TR.
Maximum Tractive Effort: 409 kN (92000 lbf).
Continuous Tractive Effort: 260 kN (58390 lbf) at 15.9 mph.
Power at Rail: 1850 kW (2480 hp).   **Train Brakes:** Air.
Brake Force: 68 t.   **Dimensions:** 21.35 x 2.64 m.
Weight: 127 t.   **Wheel Diameter:** 1120 mm.
Design Speed: 87.5 mph.   **Maximum Speed:** 75 mph.
Fuel Capacity: 6550 litres.   **Route Availability:** 7.
Train Supply: Not equipped.   **Total:** 385.

All equipped with Slow Speed Control.

Class 66s previously used in the UK but now in use abroad are listed in section 5 of this book. Some of the DBC 66s moved to France return to Great Britain from time to time for maintenance or operational requirements.

Class 66 delivery dates. The Class 66 design and delivery evolved over an 18-year period, with more than 400 locomotives delivered. For clarity the delivery dates (by year) for each batch of locomotives is as follows:

66001–250	EWS (now DB Cargo). 1998–2000 (some now in use in France or Poland and ten sold to GB Railfreight).
66301–305	Fastline. 2008. Now used by DRS.
66401–410	DRS. 2003. Now in use with GB Railfreight or Colas Rail and renumbered 66733–737 and 66742–746 (66734 since scrapped).
66411–420	DRS. 2006. Now leased by Freightliner (66411/412/417 exported to Poland).
66421–430	DRS. 2007.
66431–434	DRS. 2008
66501–505	Freightliner. 1999
66506–520	Freightliner. 2000
66521–525	Freightliner. 2000 (66521 since scrapped).
66526–531	Freightliner. 2001
66532–537	Freightliner. 2001
66538–543	Freightliner. 2001
66544–553	Freightliner. 2001
66554	Freightliner. 2002†
66555–566	Freightliner. 2002
66567–574	Freightliner. 2003. 66573–574 now used by Colas Rail and renumbered 66846–847.
66575–577	Freightliner. 2004. Now used by Colas Rail and renumbered 66848–850.
66578–581	Freightliner. 2005. Now used by GBRf and renumbered 66738–741.
66582–594	Freightliner. 2007 (66582/583/584/586 exported to Poland).
66595–599	Freightliner. 2008 (66595 exported to Poland).
66601–606	Freightliner. 2000
66607–612	Freightliner. 2002 (66607/609/611/612 exported to Poland)
66613–618	Freightliner. 2003
66619–622	Freightliner. 2005
66623–625	Freightliner. 2007 (66624/625 exported to Poland).
66701–707	GB Railfreight. 2001
66708–712	GB Railfreight. 2002
66713–717	GB Railfreight. 2003
66718–722	GB Railfreight. 2006
66723–727	GB Railfreight. 2006
66728–732	GB Railfreight. 2008
66747–749	Built in 2008 as 20078968-004/006/007 (DE 6313/15/16) for Crossrail AG in the Netherlands but never used. Sold to GB Railfreight in 2012.
66750–751	Built in 2003 as 20038513-01/04 and have worked in the Netherlands, Germany and Poland. GBRf secured these two locomotives on lease in 2013.
66752–772	GB Railfreight. 2014
66773–779	GB Railfreight. 2016
66780–789	GB Railfreight. 1998–2000. Former DBC locomotives acquired in 2017 that have been renumbered in the GBRf number series.
66951–952	Freightliner. 2004
66953–957	Freightliner. 2008 (66954 exported to Poland).

Advertising and non-standard liveries:

66623	Bardon Aggregates blue.
66709	MSC – blue with images of a container ship.
66718	London Underground 150, (black).
66720	Day and night (various colours, different on each side).
66721	London Underground 150 (white with tube map images). Also carries the number 1733.
66727	Maritime (blue).
66775	Also carries the number F231.
66779	BR dark green.
66780	Cemex (grey, blue & red).
66783	Biffa (red & orange).

Class 66/0. DB Cargo-operated locomotives.

All fitted with Swinghead Automatic "Buckeye" Combination Couplers except 66001 and 66002.

† Fitted with additional lights and drawgear for Lickey banking duties.

t Fitted with tripcocks for working over London Underground tracks between Harrow-on-the-Hill and Amersham.

66001 t	**DB**	DB	WBAR	TO	
66002	E	DB	WBAE	TO	
66003	E	DB	WBAE	TO	
66004	E	DB	WBAE	TO	
66005	E	DB	WBAT	TO	
66006	E	DB	WBAE	TO	
66007	E	DB	WBAR	TO	
66009	**DB**	DB	WBAE	TO	
66011	E	DB	WBAE	TO	
66012	E	DB	WBAE	TO	
66013	E	DB	WBAE	TO	
66014	E	DB	WBAR	TO	
66015	E	DB	WBAR	TO	
66017 t	**DB**	DB	WBAR	TO	
66018	**DB**	DB	WBAE	TO	
66019 t	**DB**	DB	WBRT	TO	
66020	**DB**	DB	WBAE	TO	
66021	**DB**	DB	WBAR	TO	
66023	E	DB	WBAT	TO	
66024	E	DB	WBAE	TO	
66025	E	DB	WBRT	TO	
66027	**DB**	DB	WBAE	TO	
66030	E	DB	WBAR	TO	
66031	E	DB	WBAT	TO	
66034	**DB**	DB	WBAE	TO	
66035	**DB**	DB	WBAE	TO	Resourceful
66037	E	DB	WBAR	TO	
66039	E	DB	WBAE	TO	
66040	E	DB	WBAR	TO	
66041	**DB**	DB	WBAE	TO	

66043	E	DB	WQAA	TO (S)	
66044	DB	DB	WBAE	TO	
66047	E	DB	WBAT	TO	
66050	E	DB	WBRT	TO	EWS Energy
66051	E	DB	WBRT	TO	
66053	E	DB	WBAE	TO	
66054	E	DB	WBAR	TO	
66055 †	DB	DB	WBAR	TO	Alain Thauvette
66056 †	E	DB	WBLE	TO	
66057 †	E	DB	WBAE	TO	
66059 †	E	DB	WBLE	TO	
66060	E	DB	WBAT	TO	
66061	E	DB	WBAE	TO	
66063	E	DB	WBAE	TO	
66065	DB	DB	WBAR	TO	
66066	DB	DB	WBAR	TO	Geoff Spencer
66067	E	DB	WBAR	TO	
66068	E	DB	WBAR	TO	
66069	E	DB	WBAR	TO	
66070	E	DB	WBAT	TO	
66074	DB	DB	WBAE	TO	
66075	E	DB	WBAT	TO	
66076	E	DB	WBAE	TO	
66077	E	DB	WBAR	TO	
66078	E	DB	WBAE	TO	
66079	E	DB	WBAR	TO	James Nightall G.C.
66080	E	DB	WBAE	TO	
66082	DB	DB	WBAE	TO	
66083	E	DB	WBAR	TO	
66084	E	DB	WBAR	TO	
66085	DB	DB	WBAR	TO	
66086	E	DB	WBAE	TO	
66087	E	DB	WBAE	TO	
66088	E	DB	WBAE	TO	
66089	E	DB	WBAR	TO	
66090	E	DB	WBAE	TO	
66091	E	DB	WBAR	TO	
66092	E	DB	WBAE	TO	
66093	E	DB	WBAE	TO	
66094	E	DB	WBAE	TO	
66095	E	DB	WBAE	TO	
66096	E	DB	WBAR	TO	
66097	DB	DB	WBAE	TO	
66098	E	DB	WBAE	TO	
66099 r	E	DB	WBBE	TO	
66100 r	E	DB	WBBE	TO	
66101 r	DB	DB	WBBE	TO	
66102 r	E	DB	WBBE	TO	
66103 r	E	DB	WBBE	TO	
66104 r	DB	DB	WBAR	TO	
66105 r	E	DB	WBAR	TO	

66106 r	E	DB	WBBE	TO	
66107 r	E	DB	WBAR	TO	
66108 r	E	DB	WBAE	TO	
66109	E	DB	WBAR	TO	
66110 r	E	DB	WBBE	TO	
66111 r	E	DB	WBBT	TO	
66112 r	E	DB	WBBE	TO	
66113 r	E	DB	WBBE	TO	
66114 r	DB	DB	WBBE	TO	
66115	DB	DB	WBRT	TO	
66116	E	DB	WBAE	TO	
66117	DB	DB	WBAE	TO	
66118	DB	DB	WBAE	TO	
66119	E	DB	WBAE	TO	
66120	E	DB	WBRT	TO	
66121	E	DB	WBRT	TO	
66122	E	DB	WBAE	TO	
66124	DB	DB	WBAR	TO	
66125	E	DB	WBAE	TO	
66126	E	DB	WBAE	TO	
66127	E	DB	WBAT	TO	
66128	DB	DB	WBAE	TO	
66129	E	DB	WBAR	TO	
66130	DB	DB	WBAR	TO	
66131	DB	DB	WBAT	TO	
66133	E	DB	WBAE	TO	
66134	E	DB	WBAE	TO	
66135	DB	DB	WBAE	TO	
66136	DB	DB	WBAE	TO	
66137	DB	DB	WBAE	TO	
66138	E	DB	WBAR	TO	
66139	E	DB	WBAE	TO	
66140	E	DB	WBAE	TO	
66142	E	DB	WBAR	TO	
66143	E	DB	WBAE	TO	
66144	E	DB	WBAR	TO	
66145	E	DB	WQAA	TO (S)	
66147	E	DB	WBAE	TO	
66148	E	DB	WQAA	TO (S)	
66149	DB	DB	WBAE	TO	
66150	DB	DB	WBAE	TO	
66151	E	DB	WBAE	TO	
66152	DB	DB	WBAE	TO	Derek Holmes Railway Operator
66154	E	DB	WBAE	TO	
66155	E	DB	WBAE	TO	
66156	E	DB	WBRT	TO	
66158	E	DB	WBAE	TO	
66160	E	DB	WBAE	TO	
66161	E	DB	WBAE	TO	
66162	E	DB	WBAR	TO	
66164	E	DB	WBAE	TO	

66165	**DB**	DB	WBAR	TO	
66167	E	DB	WBAE	TO	
66168	E	DB	WBAR	TO	
66169	E	DB	WBAR	TO	
66170	E	DB	WBAE	TO	
66171	E	DB	WBAR	TO	
66172	E	DB	WBAE	TO	PAUL MELLENEY
66174	E	DB	WBAE	TO	
66175	DB	DB	WBAE	TO	
66176	E	DB	WBAR	TO	
66177	E	DB	WBAT	TO	
66181	E	DB	WBAE	TO	
66182	E	DB	WBAE	TO	
66183	E	DB	WBAE	TO	
66185	DB	DB	WBRT	TO	DP WORLD London Gateway
66186	E	DB	WBAE	TO	
66187	E	DB	WBAE	TO	
66188	E	DB	WBRT	TO	
66192	DB	DB	WBAR	TO	
66194	E	DB	WBAR	TO	
66197	E	DB	WBAR	TO	
66198	E	DB	WBAR	TO	
66199	E	DB	WBAE	TO	
66200	E	DB	WBRT	TO	
66206	DB	DB	WBAR	TO	
66207	E	DB	WBAE	TO	
66221	E	DB	WBAT	TO	
66230	DB	DB	WQAA	TO (S)	

**Class 66/3. Former Fastline-operated locomotives now operated by DRS.
Low emission**. Details as Class 66/0 except:

Engine: EMD 12N-710G3B-T2 two stroke of 2420 kW (3245 hp) at 904 rpm.
Traction Motors: General Motors D43TRC.
Fuel Capacity: 5150 litres.

66301	DR	BN	XHIM	KM	Kingmoor TMD
66302	DR	BN	XHIM	KM	
66303	DR	BN	XHIM	KM	
66304	DR	BN	XHIM	KM	
66305	DR	BN	XHIM	KM	

Class 66/4. Low emission. Macquarie Group-owned. Details as Class 66/3.

66413	FG	MQ	DFIN	LD	
66414	FH	MQ	DFIN	LD	
66415	DS	MQ	DFIN	LD	
66416	FH	MQ	DFIN	LD	
66418	FH	MQ	DFIN	LD	PATRIOT – IN MEMORY OF FALLEN RAILWAY EMPLOYEES
66419	DS	MQ	DFIN	LD	
66420	FH	MQ	DFIN	LD	
66421	DR	MQ	XHIM	KM	Gresty Bridge TMD

66422	**DR**	MQ	XHIM	KM	
66423	**DR**	MQ	XHIM	KM	
66424	**DR**	MQ	XHIM	KM	
66425	**DR**	MQ	XHIM	KM	
66426	**DR**	MQ	XHIM	KM	
66427	**DR**	MQ	XHIM	KM	
66428	**DR**	MQ	XHIM	KM	
66429	**DR**	MQ	XHIM	KM	
66430	**DR**	MQ	XHIM	KM	
66431	**DR**	MQ	XHIM	KM	
66432	**DR**	MQ	XHIM	KM	
66433	**DR**	MQ	XHIM	KM	
66434	**DR**	MQ	XHIM	KM	

Class 66/5. Standard design. Freightliner-operated locomotives. Details as Class 66/0.

66501	**FL**	P	DFIM	LD	Japan 2001
66502	**FL**	P	DFIM	LD	Basford Hall Centenary 2001
66503	**FL**	P	DFIM	LD	The RAILWAY MAGAZINE
66504	**FH**	P	DFIM	LD	
66505	**FL**	P	DFIM	LD	
66506	**FL**	E	DFIM	LD	Crewe Regeneration
66507	**FL**	E	DFHJ	LD	
66508	**FL**	E	DFIM	LD	
66509	**FL**	E	DFIM	LD	
66510	**FL**	E	DFHJ	LD	
66511	**FL**	E	DFIM	LD	
66512	**FL**	E	DFIM	LD	
66513	**FL**	E	DFIM	LD	
66514	**FL**	E	DFIM	LD	
66515	**FL**	E	DFIM	LD	
66516	**FL**	E	DFIM	LD	
66517	**FL**	E	DFIM	LD	
66518	**FL**	E	DFIM	LD	
66519	**FL**	E	DFHJ	LD	
66520	**FL**	E	DFIM	LD	
66522	**FL**	E	DFHJ	LD	
66523	**FL**	E	DFIM	LD	
66524	**FL**	E	DFIM	LD	
66525	**FL**	E	DFIM	LD	
66526	**FL**	P	DFIM	LD	Driver Steve Dunn (George)
66528	**FH**	P	DFIM	LD	Madge Elliot MBE Borders Railway Opening 2015
66529	**FL**	P	DFIM	LD	
66531	**FL**	P	DFIM	LD	
66532	**FL**	P	DFIM	LD	P&O Nedlloyd Atlas
66533	**FL**	P	DFIM	LD	Hanjin Express/Senator Express
66534	**FL**	P	DFIM	LD	OOCL Express
66536	**FL**	P	DFIM	LD	
66537	**FL**	P	DFIM	LD	
66538	**FL**	E	DFIM	LD	

66539	FL	E	DFIM	LD	
66540	FL	E	DFIM	LD	Ruby
66541	FL	E	DFIM	LD	
66542	FL	E	DFIM	LD	
66543	FL	E	DFIM	LD	
66544	FL	P	DFIM	LD	
66545	FL	P	DFIM	LD	
66546	FL	P	DFIM	LD	
66547	FL	P	DFIM	LD	
66548	FL	P	DFIM	LD	
66549	FL	P	DFIM	LD	
66550	FL	P	DFIM	LD	
66551	FL	P	DFIM	LD	
66552	FL	P	DFIM	LD	Maltby Raider
66553	FL	P	DFIM	LD	
66554	FL	E	DFIM	LD	
66555	FL	E	DFIM	LD	
66556	FL	E	DFIM	LD	
66557	FL	E	DFIM	LD	
66558	FL	E	DFIM	LD	
66559	FL	E	DFIM	LD	
66560	FL	E	DFIM	LD	
66561	FL	E	DFIM	LD	
66562	FL	E	DFIM	LD	
66563	FL	E	DFIM	LD	
66564	FL	E	DFIM	LD	
66565	FL	E	DFIM	LD	
66566	FL	E	DFIM	LD	
66567	FL	E	DFIM	LD	
66568	FL	E	DFIM	LD	
66569	FL	E	DFIM	LD	
66570	FL	E	DFIM	LD	
66571	FL	E	DFIM	LD	
66572	FL	E	DFIM	LD	

Class 66/5. Freightliner-operated low emission locomotives. Details as Class 66/3.

66585	FL	MQ	DFIN	LD	
66587	FL	MQ	DFIN	LD	
66588	FL	MQ	DFIN	LD	
66589	FL	MQ	DFIN	LD	
66590	FL	MQ	DFIN	LD	
66591	FL	MQ	DFIN	LD	
66592	FL	MQ	DFIN	LD	Johnson Stevens Agencies
66593	FL	MQ	DFIN	LD	3MG MERSEY MULTIMODAL GATEWAY
66594	FL	MQ	DFIN	LD	NYK Spirit of Kyoto
66596	FL	BN	DFIN	LD	
66597	FL	BN	DFIN	LD	Viridor
66598	FL	BN	DFIN	LD	
66599	FL	BN	DFIN	LD	

Class 66/6. Freightliner-operated locomotives with modified gear ratios.
Details as Class 66/0 except:

Maximum Tractive Effort: 467 kN (105080 lbf).
Continuous Tractive Effort: 296 kN (66630 lbf) at 14.0 mph.
Design Speed: 65 mph.   **Maximum Speed:** 65 mph.

66601	**FL**	P	DFHH	LD	The Hope Valley
66602	**FL**	P	DFHH	LD	
66603	**FL**	P	DFHH	LD	
66604	**FL**	P	DFHH	LD	
66605	**FL**	P	DFHH	LD	
66606	**FL**	P	DFHH	LD	
66607	**FL**	P	DFHH	LD	
66610	**FL**	P	DFHH	LD	
66613	**FL**	E	DFHH	LD	
66614	**FL**	E	DFHH	LD	1916 POPPY 2016
66615	**FL**	E	DFHH	LD	
66616	**FL**	E	DFHH	LD	
66617	**FL**	E	DFHH	LD	
66618	**FL**	E	DFHH	LD	Railways Illustrated Annual Photographic Awards Alan Barnes
66619	**FL**	E	DFHH	LD	Derek W. Johnson MBE
66620	**FL**	E	DFHH	LD	
66621	**FL**	E	DFHH	LD	
66622	**FL**	E	DFHH	LD	

Class 66/6. Freightliner-operated low emission locomotive with modified gear ratios. Details as Class 66/6 except:

Fuel Capacity: 5150 litres.

66623	**0**	MQ	DFHH	LD	Bill Bolsover

Class 66/7. Standard design. GB Railfreight-operated locomotives. Details as Class 66/0.

66701	**GB**	E	GBBT	RR	
66702	**GB**	E	GBBT	RR	Blue Lightning
66703	**GB**	E	GBBT	RR	Doncaster PSB 1981–2002
66704	**GB**	E	GBBT	RR	Colchester Power Signalbox
66705	**GB**	E	GBBT	RR	Golden Jubilee
66706	**GB**	E	GBBT	RR	Nene Valley
66707	**GB**	E	GBBT	RR	Sir Sam Fay GREAT CENTRAL RAILWAY
66708	**GB**	E	GBBT	RR	Jayne
66709	**AL**	E	GBBT	RR	Sorrento
66710	**GB**	E	GBBT	RR	Phil Packer BRIT
66711	**Al**	E	GBBT	RR	Sence
66712	**GB**	E	GBBT	RR	Peterborough Power Signalbox
66713	**GB**	E	GBBT	RR	Forest City
66714	**GB**	E	GBBT	RR	Cromer Lifeboat
66715	**GB**	E	GBBT	RR	VALOUR – IN MEMORY OF ALL RAILWAY EMPLOYEES WHO GAVE THEIR LIVES FOR THEIR COUNTRY

| 66716 | **GB** E | GBBT | RR | LOCOMOTIVE & CARRIAGE INSTITUTION CENTENARY 1911–2011 |
| 66717 | **GB** E | GBBT | RR | Good Old Boy |

66718–751. GB Railfreight locomotives.

Details as Class 66/0 except 66718–732/747–749 as below:

Engine: EMD 12N-710G3B-T2 two stroke of 2420 kW (3245 hp) at 904 rpm.
Traction Motors: General Motors D43TRC.
Fuel Capacity: 5546 litres (66718–722) or 5150 litres (66723–732/747–749).

66747–749 were originally built for Crossrail AG in the Netherlands.

66750/751 were originally built for mainland Europe in 2003.

66718	**AL** E	GBLT	RR	Sir Peter Hendy CBE
66719	**GB** E	GBLT	RR	METRO-LAND
66720	**0** E	GBLT	RR	
66721	**AL** E	GBLT	RR	Harry Beck
66722	**GB** E	GBLT	RR	Sir Edward Watkin
66723	**GB** E	GBLT	RR	Chinook
66724	**GB** E	GBLT	RR	Drax Power Station
66725	**GB** E	GBLT	RR	SUNDERLAND
66726	**GB** E	GBLT	RR	SHEFFIELD WEDNESDAY
66727	**AL** E	GBLT	RR	Maritime One
66728	**GB** P	GBLT	RR	Institution of Railway Operators
66729	**GB** P	GBLT	RR	DERBY COUNTY
66730	**GB** P	GBLT	RR	Whitemoor
66731	**GB** P	GBLT	RR	interhub GB
66732	**GB** P	GBLT	RR	GBRf The First Decade 1999–2009 John Smith – MD

66733	(66401) r	**GB** P	GBFM	RR	Cambridge PSB
66735	(66403)	**GB** P	GBBT	RR	
66736	(66404) r	**GB** P	GBFM	RR	WOLVERHAMPTON WANDERERS
66737	(66405) r	**GB** P	GBFM	RR	Lesia
66738	(66578) r	**GB** BN	GBBT	RR	HUDDERSFIELD TOWN
66739	(66579)	**GB** BN	GBFM	RR	Bluebell Railway
66740	(66580) r	**GB** BN	GBFM	RR	Sarah
66741	(66581)	**GB** BN	GBBT	RR	Swanage Railway

| 66742 | (66406, 66841) | **GB** BN | GBBT | RR | ABP Port of Immingham Centenary 1912–2012 |

66743	(66407, 66842) r	**M** BN	GBFM	RR	
66744	(66408, 66843)	**GB** BN	GBBT	RR	Crossrail
66745	(66409, 66844)	**GB** BN	GBRT	RR	Modern Railways The first 50 years

| 66746 | (66410, 66845) r | **M** BN | GBFM | RR | |

66747	(20078968-007)	**GB** GB	GBEB	RR	
66748	(20078968-004)	**GB** GB	GBEB	RR	West Burton 50
66749	(20078968-006)	**GB** GB	GBEB	RR	
66750	(20038513-01)	**GB** BN	GBEB	RR	Bristol Panel Signal Box

66751 (20038513-04) c **GB** BN GBEB   RR   Inspiration Delivered
Hitachi Rail Europe

66752–779. Low emission. New build locomotives. Details as Class 66/3.

66752	**GB**	GB	GBEL	RR	The Hoosier State
66753	**GB**	GB	GBEL	RR	EMD Roberts Road
66754	**GB**	GB	GBEL	RR	Northampton Saints
66755	**GB**	GB	GBEL	RR	Tony Berkeley OBE
					RFG Chairman 1997–2018
66756	**GB**	GB	GBEL	RR	Royal Corps of Signals
66757	**GB**	GB	GBEL	RR	West Somerset Railway
66758	**GB**	GB	GBEL	RR	The Pavior
66759	**GB**	GB	GBEL	RR	Chippy
66760	**GB**	GB	GBEL	RR	David Gordon Harris
66761	**GB**	GB	GBEL	RR	Wensleydale Railway Association
					25 Years 1990–2015
66762	**GB**	GB	GBEL	RR	
66763	**GB**	GB	GBEL	RR	Severn Valley Railway
66764	**GB**	GB	GBEL	RR	
66765	**GB**	GB	GBEL	RR	
66766	**GB**	GB	GBEL	RR	
66767	**GB**	GB	GBEL	RR	
66768	**GB**	GB	GBEL	RR	
66769	**GB**	GB	GBEL	RR	
66770	**GB**	GB	GBEL	RR	
66771	**GB**	GB	GBEL	RR	
66772	**GB**	GB	GBEL	RR	
66773	**GB**	GB	GBNB	RR	
66774	**GB**	GB	GBNB	RR	
66775	**GB**	GB	GBNB	RR	HMS Argyll
66776	**GB**	GB	GBNB	RR	Joanne
66777	**GB**	GB	GBNB	RR	Annette
66778	**GB**	GB	GBNB	RR	Darius Cheskin
66779	**0**	GB	GBEL	RR	EVENING STAR

66780–789. Standard design. Former DB Cargo locomotives acquired by GB Railfreight in 2017. Details as Class 66/0. Fitted with Swinghead Automatic "Buckeye" Combination Couplers.

† Fitted with additional lights and drawgear formerly used for Lickey banking duties.

66780 (66008)	**AL**	GB	GBOB	RR	
66781 (66016)	**GB**	GB	GBOB	RR	
66782 (66046)	**GB**	GB	GBOB	RR	
66783 (66058) †	**AL**	GB	GBOB	RR	The Flying Dustman
66784 (66081)	**GB**	GB	GBOB	RR	Keighley & Worth Valley
					Railway 50th Anniversary
					1968–2018
66785 (66132)	**GB**	GB	GBOB	RR	
66786 (66141)	**GB**	GB	GBOB	RR	
66787 (66184)	**GB**	GB	GBOB	RR	

| 66788 | (66238) | **GB** | GB | GBOB | RR | |
| 66789 | (66250) | **BL** | GB | GBOB | RR | British Rail 1948–1997 |

Class 66/8. Standard design. Colas Rail locomotives. Details as Class 66/0.

66846	(66573)	**CS**	CS	COLO	HJ	
66847	(66574)	**CS**	CS	COLO	HJ	
66848	(66575)	**CS**	CS	COLO	HJ	
66849	(66576)	**CS**	CS	COLO	HJ	Wylam Dilly
66850	(66577)	**CS**	CS	COLO	HJ	David Maidment OBE

Class 66/9. Freightliner locomotives. Low emission "demonstrator" locomotives. Details as Class 66/3.

* **Fuel Capacity:** 5905 litres.

| 66951 | * | **FL** | E | DFIN | LD | |
| 66952 | | **FL** | E | DFIN | LD | |

Class 66/5. Freightliner-operated low emission locomotives. Owing to the 665xx number range being full, subsequent deliveries of 66/5s were numbered from 66953 onwards. Details as Class 66/5 (low emission).

66953	**FL**	BN	DFIN	LD	
66955	**FL**	BN	DFIN	LD	
66956	**FL**	BN	DFIN	LD	
66957	**FL**	BN	DFIN	LD	Stephenson Locomotive Society 1909–2009

CLASS 67   ALSTOM/GENERAL MOTORS   Bo-Bo

Built: 1999–2000 by Alstom at Valencia, Spain, as sub-contractors for General Motors (General Motors model JT42 HW-HS).
Engine: GM 12N-710G3B-EC two stroke of 2385 kW (3200 hp) at 904 rpm.
Main Alternator: General Motors AR9A/HEP7/CA6C.
Traction Motors: General Motors D43FM.
Maximum Tractive Effort: 141 kN (31770 lbf).
Continuous Tractive Effort: 90 kN (20200 lbf) at 46.5 mph.
Power at Rail: 1860 kW.   **Train Brakes:** Air.
Brake Force: 78 t.   **Dimensions:** 19.74 x 2.72 m.
Weight: 90 t.   **Wheel Diameter:** 965 mm.
Design Speed: 125 mph.   **Maximum Speed:** 125 mph (* 80 mph).
Fuel Capacity: 4927 litres.   **Route Availability:** 8.
Train Supply: Electric, index 66.   **Total:** 30.

All equipped with Slow Speed Control and Swinghead Automatic "Buckeye" Combination Couplers.

67004, 67007, 67009 and 67011 were fitted with cast iron brake blocks for working the Fort William Sleeper.

Non-standard liveries:

67026 Diamond Jubilee silver.
67029 All over silver with DB logos.

67001	**AB**	DB	WQAA	TO (S)	
67002	**AB**	DB	WAAC	CE	
67003	**AB**	DB	WAAC	CE	
67004 r*	**AB**	DB	WABC	CE	
67005	**RZ**	DB	WAAC	CE	Queen's Messenger
67006	**RZ**	DB	WAAC	CE	Royal Sovereign
67007 r*	**E**	DB	WABC	CE	
67008	**E**	DB	WQAA	CE (S)	
67009 r*	**E**	DB	WQBA	CE (S)	
67010	**DB**	DB	WAAC	CE	
67011 r*	**E**	DB	WQBA	CE (S)	
67012	**CM**	DB	WAAC	CE	
67013	**DB**	DB	WAWC	CE	
67014	**CM**	DB	WAWC	CE	
67015	**DB**	DB	WAAC	CE	
67016	**E**	DB	WAWC	CE	
67017	**E**	DB	WQBA	CE (S)	Arrow
67018	**DB**	DB	WAAC	CE	Keith Heller
67019	**E**	DB	WQBA	TO (S)	
67020	**E**	DB	WAAC	CE	
67021	**PC**	DB	WAAC	CE	
67022	**E**	DB	WAAC	CE	
67023	**CS**	CS	COTS	RU	Stella
67024	**PC**	DB	WAAC	CE	
67025	**E**	DB	WQBA	CE (S)	Western Star
67026	**O**	DB	WQBA	CE (S)	Diamond Jubilee
67027	**CS**	CS	COTS	RU	Charlotte
67028	**DB**	DB	WAAC	CE	
67029	**O**	DB	WAWC	CE	Royal Diamond
67030 r	**E**	DB	WABC	CE	

CLASS 68   VOSSLOH/STADLER   Bo-Bo

New Vossloh/Stadler mixed-traffic locomotives now in service with DRS.

Built: 2012–16 by Vossloh/Stadler, Valencia, Spain.
Engine: Caterpillar C175-16 of 2800 kW (3750 hp) at 1740 rpm.
Main Alternator: ABB WGX560.
Traction Motors: 4 x AC frame mounted ABB 4FRA6063.
Maximum Tractive Effort: 317 kN (71260 lbf).
Continuous Tractive Effort: 250 kN (56200 lbf) at 20.5 mph.

Power at Rail:	**Train Brakes:** Air.
Brake Force: 73 t.	**Dimensions:** 20.50 x 2.69 m.
Weight: 85 t.	**Wheel Diameter:** 1100 mm.
Design Speed: 100 mph.	**Maximum Speed:** 100 mph.
Fuel Capacity: 6000 litres.	**Route Availability:** 7.
Train Supply: Electric, index 96.	**Total:** 34.

68008–015 have been modified to operate in push-pull mode on the Chiltern
Railways locomotive-hauled sets.
68019–034 have been modified to operate with the new TransPennine
Express Mark 5A stock from late 2018.

68001	**DI**	BN	XHVE	CR	Evolution
68002	**DI**	BN	XHVE	CR	Intrepid
68003	**DI**	BN	XHVE	CR	Astute
68004	**DI**	BN	XHVE	CR	Rapid
68005	**DI**	BN	XHVE	CR	Defiant
68006	**SR**	BN	XHVE	CR	Daring
68007	**SR**	BN	XHVE	CR	Valiant
68008	**DI**	BN	XHVE	CR	Avenger
68009	**DI**	BN	XHVE	CR	Titan
68010	**CM**	BN	XHCE	CR	Oxford Flyer
68011	**CM**	BN	XHCE	CR	
68012	**CM**	BN	XHCE	CR	
68013	**CM**	BN	XHCE	CR	
68014	**CM**	BN	XHCE	CR	
68015	**CM**	BN	XHCE	CR	
68016	**DI**	BN	XHVE	CR	Fearless
68017	**DI**	BN	XHVE	CR	Hornet
68018	**DI**	BN	XHVE	CR	Vigilant
68019	**TP**	BN	XHTP	CR	Brutus
68020	**TP**	BN	XHTP	CR	Reliance
68021	**TP**	BN	XHTP	CR	Tireless
68022	**TP**	BN	XHTP	CR	Resolution
68023	**TP**	BN	XHTP	CR	Achilles
68024	**TP**	BN	XHTP	CR	Centaur
68025	**TP**	BN	XHTP	CR	Superb
68026	**TP**	BN	XHTP	CR	
68027	**TP**	BN	XHTP	CR	
68028	**TP**	BN	XHTP	CR	Lord President
68029	**TP**	BN	XHTP	CR	
68030	**TP**	BN	XHTP	CR	
68031	**TP**	BN	XHTP	CR	
68032	**TP**	BN	XHTP	CR	
68033	**DI**	DR	XHVE	CR	
68034	**DI**	DR	XHVE	CR	

CLASS 70   GENERAL ELECTRIC   Co-Co

GE "PowerHaul" locomotives. 70012 was badly damaged whilst being unloaded in 2011 and was returned to Pennsylvania.

70801 (built as 70099) is a Turkish-built demonstrator that arrived in Britain in 2012. Colas Rail leased this locomotive and then in 2013 ordered a further nine locomotives (70802–810) that were delivered in 2014. 70811–817 followed in 2017.

Built: 2009–17 by General Electric, Erie, Pennsylvania, USA or by TÜLOMSAS, Eskişehir, Turkey (70801).
Engine: General Electric PowerHaul P616LDA1 of 2848 kW (3820 hp) at 1500 rpm.
Main Alternator: General Electric GTA series.
Traction Motors: AC-GE 5GEB30.

Maximum Tractive Effort: 544 kN (122000 lbf).
Continuous Tractive Effort: 427 kN (96000 lbf) at ?? mph.

Power at Rail:	**Train Brakes:** Air.
Brake Force: 96.7 t.	**Dimensions:** 21.71 x 2.64 m.
Weight: 129 t.	**Wheel Diameter:** 1066 mm.
Design Speed: 75 mph.	**Maximum Speed:** 75 mph.
Fuel Capacity: 6000 litres.	**Route Availability:** 7.
Train Supply: Not equipped.	**Total:** 36.

Class 70/0. Freightliner locomotives.

70001	**FH**	MQ	DHLT	LD (S)	PowerHaul
70002	**FH**	MQ	DHLT	LD (S)	
70003	**FH**	MQ	DFGI	LD	
70004	**FH**	MQ	DHLT	LD (S)	The Coal Industry Society
70005	**FH**	MQ	DFGI	LD	
70006	**FH**	MQ	DFGI	LD	
70007	**FH**	MQ	DFGI	LD	
70008	**FH**	MQ	DFGI	LD	
70009	**FH**	MQ	DHLT	LD (S)	
70010	**FH**	MQ	DHLT	LD (S)	
70011	**FH**	MQ	DHLT	LD (S)	
70013	**FH**	MQ	DHLT	LD (S)	
70014	**FH**	MQ	DFGI	LD	
70015	**FH**	MQ	DHLT	LD (S)	
70016	**FH**	MQ	DHLT	LD (S)	
70017	**FH**	MQ	DHLT	LD (S)	
70018	**FH**	MQ	DHLT	LD (S)	
70019	**FH**	MQ	DHLT	LD (S)	
70020	**FH**	MQ	DFGI	LD	

Class 70/8. Colas Rail locomotives.

70801	**CS**	LF	COLO	CF
70802	**CS**	LF	COLO	CF
70803	**CS**	LF	COLO	CF
70804	**CS**	LF	COLO	CF
70805	**CS**	LF	COLO	CF
70806	**CS**	LF	COLO	CF
70807	**CS**	LF	COLO	CF
70808	**CS**	LF	COLO	CF
70809	**CS**	LF	COLO	CF
70810	**CS**	LF	COLO	CF
70811	**CS**	CS	COLO	CF
70812	**CS**	CS	COLO	CF
70813	**CS**	CS	COLO	CF
70814	**CS**	CS	COLO	CF
70815	**CS**	CS	COLO	CF
70816	**CS**	CS	COLO	CF
70817	**CS**	CS	COLO	CF

2. ELECTRO-DIESEL &
ELECTRIC LOCOMOTIVES

CLASS 73/1   BR/ENGLISH ELECTRIC   Bo-Bo

Electro-diesel locomotives which can operate either from a DC supply or using power from a diesel engine.

Built: 1965–67 by English Electric Co. at Vulcan Foundry, Newton-le-Willows.
Engine: English Electric 4SRKT of 447 kW (600 hp) at 850 rpm.
Main Generator: English Electric 824/5D.
Electric Supply System: 750 V DC from third rail.
Traction Motors: English Electric 546/1B.
Maximum Tractive Effort (Electric): 179 kN (40000 lbf).
Maximum Tractive Effort (Diesel): 160 kN (36000 lbf).
Continuous Rating (Electric): 1060 kW (1420 hp) giving a tractive effort of 35 kN (7800 lbf) at 68 mph.
Continuous Tractive Effort (Diesel): 60 kN (13600 lbf) at 11.5 mph.
Maximum Rail Power (Electric): 2350 kW (3150 hp) at 42 mph.
Train Brakes: Air, vacuum & electro-pneumatic († Air & electro-pneumatic).
Brake Force: 31 t.   **Dimensions:** 16.36 x 2.64 m.
Weight: 77 t.   **Wheel Diameter:** 1016 mm.
Design Speed: 90 mph.   **Maximum Speed:** 90 mph.
Fuel Capacity: 1409 litres.   **Route Availability:** 6.
Train Supply: Electric, index 66 (on electric power only). **Total:** 30.

Formerly numbered E6007–E6020/E6022–E6026/E6028–E6049 (not in order).

Locomotives numbered in the 732xx series are classed as 73/2 and were originally dedicated to Gatwick Express services.

There have been two separate Class 73 rebuild projects. For GBRf 11 locomotives were rebuilt at Brush, Loughborough with a 1600 hp MTU engine (renumbered 73961–971). For Network Rail 73104/211 were rebuilt at RVEL Derby (now Loram) with 2 x QSK19 750 hp engines (now 73951/952).

Non-standard liveries and numbering:

73110   Carries original number E6016.
73128   Two-tone grey.
73139   Light blue & light grey.
73235   Plain dark blue.

73101	**PC**	GB	GBED	ZG (S)
73107	**GB**	GB	GBED	SE	Tracy
73109	**GB**	GB	GBED	SE
73110	**B**	GB	GBBR	ZG (S)
73119	**GB**	GB	GBED	SE	Borough of Eastleigh
73128	**GB**	GB	GBED	SE	O.V.S. BULLEID C.B.E.
73133	**TT**	TT	MBED	ZG
73134	**IC**	GB	GBBR	LB (S)	Woking Homes 1885–1985

73136	**GB**	GB	GBED	SE	Mhairi
73138	**Y**	NR	QADD	ZA	
73139	**O**	GB	GBED	ZG (S)	
73141	**GB**	GB	GBED	SE	Charlotte
73201 †	**B**	GB	GBED	SE	Broadlands
73202 †	**SN**	P	MBED	SL	Graham Stenning
73212 †	**GB**	GB	GBED	SE	Fiona
73213 †	**GB**	GB	GBED	SE	Rhodalyn
73235 †	**O**	P	HYWD	BM	

CLASS 73/9 (RVEL)   BR/RVEL   Bo-Bo

The 7395x number series is reserved for rebuilt Network Rail locomotives.

Rebuilt: Re-engineered by RVEL Derby 2013–15.
Engine: 2 x QSK19 of 560 kW (750 hp) at 1800 rpm (total 1120 kw (1500 hp)).
Main Alternator: 2 x Marathon Magnaplus.
Electric Supply System: 750 V DC from third rail.
Traction Motors: English Electric 546/1B.
Maximum Tractive Effort (Electric): 179 kN (40000 lbf).
Maximum Tractive Effort (Diesel): 179 kN (40000 lbf).
Continuous Rating (Electric): 1060 kW (1420 hp) giving a tractive effort of 35 kN (7800 lbf) at 68 mph.
Continuous Tractive Effort (Diesel): 990 kW (1328 hp) giving a tractive effort of 33 kN (7420 lbf) at 68 mph.
Maximum Rail Power (Electric): 2350 kW (3150 hp) at 42 mph.

Train Brakes: Air.	**Brake Force:** 31 t.
Weight: 77 t.	**Dimensions:** 16.36 x 2.64 m.
Maximum Speed: 90 mph.	**Wheel Diameter:** 1016 mm.
Fuel Capacity: 2260 litres.	**Route Availability:** 6.
Train Supply: Not equipped.	

73951	(73104)	**Y**	LO	QADD	ZA	Malcolm Brinded
73952	(73211)	**Y**	LO	QADD	ZA	Janis Kong

CLASS 73/9 (GBRf)   BR/BRUSH   Bo-Bo

GBRf Class 73s rebuilt at Brush Loughborough. 73961–965 are normally used on Network Rail contracts and 73966–971 are used by Caledonian Sleeper.

Rebuilt: Re-engineered by Brush, Loughborough 2014–16.
Engine: MTU 8V4000 R43L of 1195 kW (1600 hp) at 1800 rpm.
Main Alternator: Lechmotoren SDV 87.53-12.
Electric Supply System: 750 V DC from third rail (73961–965 only).
Traction Motors: English Electric 546/1B.
Maximum Tractive Effort (Electric): 179 kN (40000 lbf).
Maximum Tractive Effort (Diesel): 179 kN (40000 lbf).
Continuous Rating (Electric): 1060 kW (1420 hp) giving a tractive effort of 35 kN (7800 lbf) at 68 mph.
Continuous Tractive Effort (Diesel):
Maximum Rail Power (Electric): 2350 kW (3150 hp) at 42 mph.

Train Brakes: Air.	**Brake Force:** 31 t.

Weight: 77 t.   **Dimensions:** 16.36 x 2.64 m.
Maximum Speed: 90 mph.   **Wheel Diameter:** 1016 mm.
Fuel Capacity: 1409 litres.   **Route Availability:** 6.
Train Supply: Electric, index 38 (electric & diesel).

73961	(73209)		**GB**	GB	GBNR	SE	Alison
73962	(73204)		**GB**	GB	GBNR	SE	Dick Mabbutt
73963	(73206)		**GB**	GB	GBNR	SE	Janice
73964	(73205)		**GB**	GB	GBNR	SE	Jeanette
73965	(73208)		**GB**	GB	GBNR	SE	

73966–971 have been rebuilt for Caledonian Sleeper but their third rail electric capability has been retained. They have a higher Train Supply index and a slightly higher fuel capacity. Details as 73961–965 except:
Fuel Capacity: 1509 litres.   **Train Supply:** Electric, index 96.

73005 and 73006 were originally assembled at Eastleigh Works.

73966	(73005)	d	**CA**	GB	GBCS	EC
73967	(73006)	d	**CA**	GB	GBCS	EC
73968	(73117)	d	**CA**	GB	GBCS	EC
73969	(73105)	d	**CA**	GB	GBCS	EC
73970	(73103)	d	**CA**	GB	GBCS	EC
73971	(73207)	d	**CA**	GB	GBCS	EC

CLASS 86   BR/ENGLISH ELECTRIC   Bo-Bo

Built: 1965–66 by English Electric Co at Vulcan Foundry, Newton-le-Willows or by BR at Doncaster Works.
Electric Supply System: 25 kV AC 50 Hz overhead.
Traction Motors: AEI 282BZ axle hung.
Maximum Tractive Effort: 207 kN (46500 lbf).
Continuous Rating: 3010 kW (4040 hp) giving a tractive effort of 85 kN (19200 lbf) at 77.5 mph.
Maximum Rail Power: 4550 kW (6100 hp) at 49.5 mph.
Train Brakes: Air.   **Brake Force:** 40 t.
Dimensions: 17.83 x 2.65 m.   **Weight:** 83–86.8 t.
Wheel Diameter: 1156 mm.   **Train Supply:** Electric, index 74.
Design Speed: 110–125 mph.   **Maximum Speed:** 100 mph.
Route Availability: 6.   **Total:** 21.

Formerly numbered E3101–E3200 (not in order).

Class 86s exported for use abroad are listed in section 5 of this book.

Class 86/1. Class 87-type bogies & motors. Details as above except:

Traction Motors: GEC 412AZ frame mounted.
Maximum Tractive Effort: 258 kN (58000 lbf).
Continuous Rating: 3730 kW (5000 hp) giving a tractive effort of 95 kN (21300 lbf) at 87 mph.
Maximum Rail Power: 5860 kW (7860 hp) at 50.8 mph.
Wheel Diameter: 1150 mm.
Design Speed: 110 mph.   **Maximum Speed:** 110 mph.

86101	**CA**	EL	GBCH	WN	Sir William A Stanier FRS

Class 86/2. Standard design rebuilt with resilient wheels & Flexicoil suspension. Details as in main class heading.

Non-standard livery:

86259 BR "Electric blue". Also carries number E3137.

86229	**V**	FL	EPEX	CB (S)	
86251	**V**	FL	EPEX	CB (S)	
86259 x	**0**	PP	MBEL	WN	Les Ross/Peter Pan

Class 86/4. Details as Class 86/2 except:

Traction Motors: AEI 282AZ axle hung.
Maximum Tractive Effort: 258 kN (58000 lbf).
Continuous Rating: 2680 kW (3600 hp) giving a tractive effort of 89kN (20000lbf) at 67 mph.
Maximum Rail Power: 4400 kW (5900 hp) at 38 mph.
Weight: 83–83.9 t.
Design Speed: 100 mph.   **Maximum Speed:** 100 mph.

86401	**CA**	EL	GBCH	WN	Mons Meg

Class 86/6. Freightliner-operated locomotives.

Previously numbered in the Class 86/0 and 86/4 series'. 86608 was also regeared and renumbered 86501 between 2000 and 2016.

Details as Class 86/4 except:
Traction Motors: AEI 282AZ axle hung.
Maximum Speed: 75 mph.   **Train Supply:** Electric, isolated.

86604	**FL**	FL	DFNC	CB
86605	**FL**	FL	DFNC	CB
86607	**FL**	FL	DFNC	CB
86608	**FL**	FL	DFNC	CB
86609	**FL**	FL	DFNC	CB
86610	**FL**	FL	DFNC	CB
86612	**FL**	FL	DFNC	CB
86613	**FL**	FL	DFNC	CB
86614	**FL**	FL	DFNC	CB
86622	**FH**	FL	DFNC	CB
86627	**FL**	FL	DFNC	CB
86628	**FL**	FL	DFNC	CB
86632	**FL**	FL	DFNC	CB
86637	**FH**	FL	DFNC	CB
86638	**FL**	FL	DFNC	CB
86639	**FL**	FL	DFNC	CB

CLASS 87   BREL/GEC   Bo-Bo

Built: 1973–75 by BREL at Crewe Works.
Electric Supply System: 25 kV AC 50 Hz overhead.
Traction Motors: GEC G412AZ frame mounted.
Maximum Tractive Effort: 258 kN (58000 lbf).

Continuous Rating: 3730 kW (5000 hp) giving a tractive effort of 95 kN (21300 lbf) at 87 mph.
Maximum Rail Power: 5860 kW (7860 hp) at 50.8 mph.
Train Brakes: Air.   **Brake Force:** 40 t.
Dimensions: 17.83 x 2.65 m.   **Weight:** 83.3 t.
Wheel Diameter: 1150 mm.   **Train Supply:** Electric, index 95.
Design Speed: 110 mph.   **Maximum Speed:** 110 mph.
Route Availability: 6.   **Total:** 1.

Class 87s exported for use abroad are listed in section 5 of this book.

| 87002 | **CA** EL | GBCH | WN | Royal Sovereign |

CLASS 88   VOSSLOH/STADLER   Bo-Bo

Ten new Vossloh/Stadler bi-mode locomotives for DRS.

Built: 2015–16 by Vossloh/Sladler, Valencia, Spain.
Electric Supply System: 25 kV AC 50 Hz overhead.
Engine: Caterpillar C27 12-cylinder 708 kW (950 hp) at 1750 rpm.
Main Alternator: ABB AMXL400.
Traction Motors: ABB AMXL400.
Maximum Tractive Effort (Electric): 317 kN (71 260 lbf).
Maximum Tractive Effort (Diesel): 317 kN (71 260 lbf).
Continuous Rating: 4000 kW (5360 hp) giving a tractive effort of 250 kN (56200 lbf) at 28 mph (electric) or 4.5 mph (diesel).
Maximum Rail Power:
Train Brakes: Air, regenerative & rheostatic.
Brake Force: 73 t.   **Dimensions:** 20.50 x 2.69 m.
Weight: 85 t.   **Wheel Diameter:** 1100 mm.
Fuel Capacity: 1800 litres.   **Train Supply:** Electric, index 96.
Design Speed: 100 mph.   **Maximum Speed:** 100 mph.
Route Availability: 7.   **Total:** 10.

88001	**DI**	BN	XHVE	KM	Revolution
88002	**DI**	BN	XHVE	KM	Prometheus
88003	**DI**	BN	XHVE	KM	Genesis
88004	**DI**	BN	XHVE	KM	Pandora
88005	**DI**	BN	XHVE	KM	Minerva
88006	**DI**	BN	XHVE	KM	Juno
88007	**DI**	BN	XHVE	KM	Electra
88008	**DI**	BN	XHVE	KM	Ariadne
88009	**DI**	BN	XHVE	KM	Diana
88010	**DI**	BN	XHVE	KM	Aurora

CLASS 90   GEC   Bo-Bo

Built: 1987–90 by BREL at Crewe Works (as sub-contractors for GEC).
Electric Supply System: 25 kV AC 50 Hz overhead.
Traction Motors: GEC G412CY frame mounted.
Maximum Tractive Effort: 258 kN (58000 lbf).
Continuous Rating: 3730 kW (5000 hp) giving a tractive effort of 95 kN (21300 lbf) at 87 mph.

Maximum Rail Power: 5860 kW (7860 hp) at 68.3 mph.
Train Brakes: Air.   **Dimensions:** 18.80 x 2.74 m.
Brake Force: 40 t.   **Wheel Diameter:** 1150 mm.
Weight: 84.5 t.   **Maximum Speed:** 110 mph.
Design Speed: 110 mph.   **Route Availability:** 7.
Train Supply: Electric, index 95.   **Total:** 50.

Advertising livery: 90024 Malcolm Logistics (blue).

90001 b	**GA**	P	IANA	NC	Crown Point
90002 b	**GA**	P	IANA	NC	Eastern Daily Press 1870–2010
					SERVING NORFOLK FOR 140 YEARS
90003 b	**GA**	P	IANA	NC	
90004 b	**GA**	P	IANA	NC	City of Chelmsford
90005 b	**GA**	P	IANA	NC	Vice-Admiral Lord Nelson
90006 b	**GA**	P	IANA	NC	Modern Railways Magazine/
					Roger Ford
90007 b	**GA**	P	IANA	NC	Sir John Betjeman
90008 b	**GA**	P	IANA	NC	The East Anglian
90009 b	**GA**	P	IANA	NC	
90010 b	**GA**	P	IANA	NC	
90011 b	**GA**	P	IANA	NC	East Anglian Daily Times Suffolk & Proud
90012 b	**GA**	P	IANA	NC	Royal Anglian Regiment
90013 b	**GA**	P	IANA	NC	
90014 b	**GA**	P	IANA	NC	Norfolk and Norwich Festival
90015 b	**GA**	P	IANA	NC	Colchester Castle
90016	**FL**	FL	DFLC	CB	
90017	**E**	DB	WQBA	CE (S)	
90018	**DB**	DB	WEDC	CE	The Pride of Bellshill
90019	**DB**	DB	WEDC	CE	Multimodal
90020	**E**	DB	WEDC	CE	Collingwood
90021	**FS**	DB	WQAB	CE (S)	
90022	**EG**	DB	WQBA	CE (S)	Freightconnection
90023	**E**	DB	WQBA	CE (S)	
90024	**AL**	DB	WEAC	CE	
90025	**F**	DB	WQBA	CE (S)	
90026	**E**	DB	WQAB	CE (S)	
90027	**F**	DB	WQBA	CE (S)	Allerton T&RS Depot
90028	**E**	DB	WEDC	CE	
90029	**DB**	DB	WEDC	CE	
90030	**E**	DB	WQBA	CE (S)	
90031	**E**	DB	WQBA	CE (S)	The Railway Children Partnership
					Working For Street Children Worldwide
90032	**E**	DB	WQBA	CE (S)	
90033	**FE**	DB	WQBA	CE (S)	
90034	**DR**	DB	WEDC	CE	
90035	**E**	DB	WEAC	CE	
90036	**DB**	DB	WEDC	CE	Driver Jack Mills
90037	**E**	DB	WEAC	CE	Spirit of Dagenham
90038	**FE**	DB	WQBA	CE (S)	
90039	**E**	DB	WEDC	CE	
90040	**DB**	DB	WEAC	CE	

▲ The first Class 60 to be outshopped in GB Railfreight livery, 60095, stands at Eastleigh Works on 28/09/18. **Carl Watson**

▼ Carrying the new Freightliner livery, 66413 passes Burbage Common, Hinckley, with 4L93 10.08 Lawley Street–Felixstowe on 31/08/18. **Ian Nightingale**

▲ GB Railfreight-liveried 66714 passes Lincoln Central with 6E88 12.24 Middleton Towers–Goole sand train on 02/07/18. **Robert Pritchard**

▼ DB Cargo-liveried 67010 is seen between Frodsham and Helsby with the 16.50 Manchester Piccadilly–Llandudno on 29/08/18. **Terry Eyres**

▲ TransPennine Express-liveried 68020 is seen at Ashton, south of Roade on the WCML, with a 3B01 05.16 Longsight–Bletchley test run for the new TPE Mark 5A stock on 07/09/18. **Nigel Gibbs**

▲ Colas Rail-liveried 70816 passes along the Dawlish sea wall with 6B36 08.16 Moorswater–Aberthaw Cement Works on 17/05/18. **David Hunt**

▼ Rebuilt 73952 passes Longport leading a Derby RTC to Crewe test train on 04/06/18. **Cliff Beeton**

▲ Freightliner-liveried 86605 and 86614 pass Wandel with 4M11 18.14 Coatbridge–Crewe intermodal on 20/04/18. **Robin Ralston**

▼ Caledonian Sleeper-liveried 87002 arrives at London Paddington with the "GBRf 2018 Out of the Ordinary" railtour from Bridgend on 20/09/18.
Jamie Squibbs

▲ New Direct Rail Services-liveried 88005 and 88002 pass Flint with 6K41 14.58 Valley–Crewe train of nuclear flasks on 29/08/18.
Terry Eyres

▲ Greater Anglia-liveried 90009 stands at Ipswich with the 12.00 Norwich–London Liverpool Street on 06/08/18. **Robert Pritchard**

▼ Virgin Trains East Coast-liveried 91105 passes Retford with the 13.30 King's Cross–Edinburgh on 25/08/18. **Robert Pritchard**

▲ GB Railfreight-liveried 92043 stands at London Euston having brought in the stock for the Lowland Sleeper on 17/02/18. **Tim Squires**

▼ Eurotunnel Class 9/7 9721 leaves the Cheriton terminal, just before entering the Channel Tunnel, with a lorry shuttle on 05/08/18. **Robert Pritchard**

90041	**FL**	FL	DFLC	CB
90042	**FH**	FL	DFLC	CB
90043	**FH**	FL	DFLC	CB
90044	**FF**	FL	DFLC	CB
90045	**FH**	FL	DFLC	CB
90046	**FL**	FL	DFLC	CB
90047	**FF**	FL	DFLC	CB
90048	**FF**	FL	DFLC	CB
90049	**FH**	FL	DFLC	CB
90050	**FF**	AV	DHLT	CB (S)

CLASS 91   GEC   Bo-Bo

Built: 1988–91 by BREL at Crewe Works (as sub-contractors for GEC).
Electric Supply System: 25 kV AC 50 Hz overhead.
Traction Motors: GEC G426AZ.
Maximum Tractive Effort: 190 kN (43 000 lbf).
Continuous Rating: 4540 kW (6090 hp) giving a tractive effort of 170 kN at 96 mph.
Maximum Rail Power: 4700 kW (6300 hp) at ?? mph.

Train Brakes: Air.	**Dimensions:** 19.41 x 2.74 m.
Brake Force: 45 t.	**Wheel Diameter:** 1000 mm.
Weight: 84 t.	**Maximum Speed:** 125 mph.
Design Speed: 140 mph.	**Route Availability:** 7.
Train Supply: Electric, index 95.	**Total:** 31.

Locomotives were originally numbered in the 910xx series, but were renumbered upon completion of overhauls at Bombardier, Doncaster by the addition of 100 to their original number. The exception to this rule was 91023 which was renumbered 91132.

91114 has been fitted with a second pantograph for evaluation purposes.

Advertising liveries:

91101 Flying Scotsman (red, white & purple).
91110 Battle of Britain (black and grey).
91111 For the fallen (various with poppy and Union Jack vinyls).

91101	**AL**	E	IECA	BN	FLYING SCOTSMAN
91102	**VE**	E	IECA	BN	City of York
91103	**VE**	E	IECA	BN	
91104	**VE**	E	IECA	BN	
91105	**VE**	E	IECA	BN	
91106	**VE**	E	IECA	BN	
91107	**VE**	E	IECA	BN	SKYFALL
91108	**VE**	E	IECA	BN	
91109	**VE**	E	IECA	BN	Sir Bobby Robson
91110	**AL**	E	IECA	BN	BATTLE OF BRITAIN MEMORIAL FLIGHT
91111	**AL**	E	IECA	BN	For the Fallen
91112	**VE**	E	IECA	BN	
91113	**VE**	E	IECA	BN	
91114	**VE**	E	IECA	BN	Durham Cathedral

91115	**VE**	E	IECA	BN	Blaydon Races
91116	**VE**	E	IECA	BN	
91117	**VE**	E	IECA	BN	WEST RIDING LIMITED
91118	**VE**	E	IECA	BN	The Fusiliers
91119	**VE**	E	IECA	BN	Bounds Green INTERCITY Depot 1977–2017
91120	**VE**	E	IECA	BN	
91121	**VE**	E	IECA	BN	
91122	**VE**	E	IECA	BN	
91124	**VE**	E	IECA	BN	
91125	**VE**	E	IECA	BN	
91126	**VE**	E	IECA	BN	Darlington Hippodrome
91127	**VE**	E	IECA	BN	
91128	**VE**	E	IECA	BN	INTERCITY 50
91129	**VE**	E	IECA	BN	
91130	**VE**	E	IECA	BN	Lord Mayor of Newcastle
91131	**VE**	E	IECA	BN	
91132	**VE**	E	IECA	BN	

CLASS 92   BRUSH   Co-Co

Built: 1993–96 by Brush Traction at Loughborough.
Electric Supply System: 25 kV AC 50 Hz overhead or 750 V DC third rail.
Traction Motors: Asea Brown Boveri design. Model 6FRA 7059B (Asynchronous 3-phase induction motors).
Maximum Tractive Effort: 400 kN (90 000 lbf).
Continuous Rating: 5040 kW (6760 hp) on AC, 4000 kW (5360 hp) on DC.

Maximum Rail Power:	**Train Brakes:** Air.
Brake Force: 63 t.	**Dimensions:** 21.34 x 2.67 m.
Weight: 126 t.	**Wheel Diameter:** 1070 mm.
Design Speed: 140 km/h (87 mph).	**Maximum Speed:** 145 km/h (90 mph).

Train Supply: Electric, index 108 (AC), 70 (DC).
Route Availability: 7.   **Total:** 33.

* Fitted with TVM430 signalling equipment to operate on High Speed 1.

Class 92s exported for use abroad are listed in section 5 of this book.

Advertising livery: 92017 Stobart Rail (two-tone blue & white).

92004		**EG**	DB	WQBA	CE (S)	Jane Austen
92006		**EP**	GB	GBET	LB (S)	Louis Armand
92007		**EG**	DB	WQBA	CE (S)	Schubert
92008		**EG**	DB	WQBA	CE (S)	Jules Verne
92009	*	**DB**	DB	WQBA	CE (S)	Marco Polo
92010	*d	**CA**	GB	GBST	WB	
92011	*	**EG**	DB	WFBC	CE	Handel
92013		**EG**	DB	WQAA	CE (S)	Puccini
92014	d	**CA**	GB	GBSL	WB	
92015	*	**DB**	DB	WFBC	CE	
92016	*	**DB**	DB	WQAA	CE (S)	
92017		**AL**	DB	WQBA	CE (S)	Bart the Engine

92018	*d	**CA**	GB	GBST	WB
92019	*	**EG**	DB	WFBC	CE	Wagner
92020		**GB**	GB	GBSL	WB
92021		**EP**	GB	GBET	CO (S)	Purcell
92023	*d	**CA**	GB	GBST	WB
92028	d	**GB**	GB	GBSL	WB
92029		**EG**	DB	WQBA	CE (S)	Dante
92031	*	**DB**	DB	WQAB	CE (S)
92032	*	**GB**	GB	GBST	WB	IMechE Railway Division
92033	d	**CA**	GB	GBSL	WB
92035		**EP**	DB	WQBA	CE (S)	Mendelssohn
92036	*	**EG**	DB	WFBC	CE	Bertolt Brecht
92037		**EG**	DB	WQAB	CE (S)	Sullivan
92038	*d	**CA**	GB	GBST	WB
92040		**EP**	GB	GBET	CO (S)	Goethe
92041	*	**EG**	DB	WFBC	CE	Vaughan Williams
92042	*	**DB**	DB	WFBC	CE
92043	*	**GB**	GB	GBST	WB
92044	*	**EP**	GB	GBST	WB	Couperin
92045		**EP**	GB	GBET	LB (S)	Chaucer
92046		**EP**	GB	GBET	LB (S)	Sweelinck

3. EUROTUNNEL LOCOMOTIVES

DIESEL LOCOMOTIVES

0001–10 are registered on TOPS as 21901–910.

0001–0005   MaK   Bo-Bo

Channel Tunnel maintenance and rescue train locomotives.
Built: 1991–92 by MaK at Kiel, Germany (Model DE 1004).
Engine: MTU 12V396 TC 13 of 950 kW (1275 hp) at 1800 rpm.
Main Alternator: ABB.   **Traction Motors:** ABB.
Maximum Tractive Effort: 305 kN (68600 lbf).
Continuous Tractive Effort: 140 kN (31500 lbf) at 20 mph.
Power At Rail: 750 kW (1012 hp).   **Dimensions:** 14.40 x ?? m.
Brake Force: 120 kN.   **Wheel Diameter:** 1000 mm.
Train Brakes: Air.   **Weight:** 90 t.
Maximum Speed: 100 km/h.   **Design Speed:** 120 km/h.
Fuel Capacity: 3500 litres.   **Multiple Working:** Within class.
Train Supply: Not equipped.   **Signalling System:** TVM430 cab signalling.

0001	**GY**	ET	CO		0004	**GY**	ET	CO
0002	**GY**	ET	CO		0005	**GY**	ET	CO
0003	**GY**	ET	CO					

0006–0010   MaK   Bo-Bo

Channel Tunnel maintenance and rescue locomotives. Rebuilt from Netherlands Railways/DB Cargo Nederland Class 6400. 0006/07 were added to the ET fleet in 2011, and 0008–10 in 2016. 0010 is used for shunting at Coquelles.

Built: 1990–91 by MaK at Kiel, Germany (Model DE 6400).
Engine: MTU 12V396 TC 13 of 1180 kW (1580 hp) at 1800 rpm.
Main Alternator: ABB.   **Traction Motors:** ABB.
Maximum Tractive Effort: 290 kN (65200 lbf).
Continuous Tractive Effort: 140 kN (31500 lbf) at 20 mph.
Power At Rail: 750 kW (1012 hp).   **Dimensions:** 14.40 x ?? m.
Brake Force: 120 kN.   **Wheel Diameter:** 1000 mm.
Train Brakes: Air.   **Weight:** 80 t.
Maximum Speed: 120 km/h.   **Design Speed:** 120 km/h.
Fuel Capacity: 2900 litres.   **Multiple Working:** Within class.
Train Supply: Not equipped.

Not fitted with TVM 430 cab signalling so have to operate with another locomotive/s when used on HS1.

0006	(6456)	**GY**	ET	CO		0009	(6451)	**GY**	ET	CO
0007	(6457)	**GY**	ET	CO		0010	(6447)	**EB**	ET	CO
0008	(6450)	**GY**	ET	CO						

0031–0042   HUNSLET/SCHÖMA   0-4-0

Built: 1989–90 by Hunslet Engine Company at Leeds as 900 mm gauge.
Rebuilt: 1993–94 by Schöma in Germany to 1435 mm gauge.
Engine: Deutz FL10L 413FW of 170 kW (230 hp) at 2300 rpm.
Transmission: Mechanical Clark 5000 series.
Maximum Tractive Effort: **Continuous Tractive Effort:**
Power At Rail:
Brake Force: **Dimensions:** 6.63 x 2.69 m.
Weight: 26–28 t.   **Wheel Diameter:**
Design Speed: 48 km/h.   **Maximum Speed:** 50 km/h.
Fuel Capacity: **Train Brakes:** Air.
Train Supply: Not equipped.   **Multiple Working:** Not equipped.

* Rebuilt with inspection platforms to check overhead catenary.

0031		**GY**	ET	CO	FRANCES
0032		**GY**	ET	CO	ELISABETH
0033		**GY**	ET	CO	SILKE
0034		**GY**	ET	CO	AMANDA
0035		**GY**	ET	CO	MARY
0036		**GY**	ET	CO	LAURENCE
0037		**GY**	ET	CO	LYDIE
0038		**GY**	ET	CO	JENNY
0039	*	**GY**	ET	CO	PACITA
0040		**GY**	ET	CO	JILL
0041	*	**GY**	ET	CO	KIM
0042		**GY**	ET	CO	NICOLE

ELECTRIC LOCOMOTIVES

9005–9840   BRUSH/ABB   Bo-Bo-Bo

Built: 1993–2002 by Brush Traction, Loughborough.
Electric Supply System: 25 kV AC 50 Hz overhead.
Traction Motors: Asea Brown Boveri design. Asynchronous 3-phase motors.
Model 6FHA 7059 (as built). Model 6FHA 7059C (7000 kW rated locos).
Maximum Tractive Effort: 400kN (90 000 lbf).
Continuous Rating: Class 9/0: 5760 kW (7725 hp). Class 9/7 and 9/8:
7000 kW (9387 hp).

Maximum Rail Power:	**Multiple Working:** TDM system.
Brake Force: 50 t.	**Dimensions:** 22.01 x 2.97 x 4.20 m.
Weight: 136 t.	**Wheel Diameter:** 1250 mm.
Maximum Speed: 100 mph.	**Design Speed:** 100 mph.
Train Supply: Electric.	**Train Brakes:** Air.

Class 9/0 Original build locos. Built 1993–94.

9005	**EB**	ET	CO	JESSYE NORMAN
9007	**EB**	ET	CO	DAME JOAN SUTHERLAND
9011	**EB**	ET	CO	JOSÉ VAN DAM
9013	**EB**	ET	CO	MARIA CALLAS
9015	**EB**	ET	CO	LÖTSCHBERG 1913
9018	**EB**	ET	CO	WILHELMENIA FERNANDEZ
9022	**EB**	ET	CO	DAME JANET BAKER
9024	**EB**	ET	CO	GOTTHARD 1882
9026	**EB**	ET	CO	FURKATUNNEL 1982
9029	**EB**	ET	CO	THOMAS ALLEN
9033	**EB**	ET	CO	MONTSERRAT CABALLE
9036	**EB**	ET	CO	ALAIN FONDARY
9037	**EB**	ET	CO	

Class 9/7. Increased power freight shuttle locos. Built 2001–02 (9711–23 built 1998–2001 as 9101–13 and rebuilt as 9711–23 2010–12).

9701		**EB**	ET	CO
9702		**EB**	ET	CO
9703		**EB**	ET	CO
9704		**EB**	ET	CO
9705		**EB**	ET	CO
9706		**EB**	ET	CO
9707		**EB**	ET	CO

9711	(9101)	**EB**	ET	CO
9712	(9102)	**EB**	ET	CO
9713	(9103)	**EB**	ET	CO
9714	(9104)	**EB**	ET	CO
9715	(9105)	**EB**	ET	CO
9716	(9106)	**EB**	ET	CO
9717	(9107)	**EB**	ET	CO
9718	(9108)	**EB**	ET	CO

9719	(9109)	**EB**	ET	CO
9720	(9110)	**EB**	ET	CO
9721	(9111)	**EB**	ET	CO
9722	(9112)	**EB**	ET	CO
9723	(9113)	**EB**	ET	CO

Class 9/8 Locos rebuilt from Class 9/0 by adding 800 to the loco number. Uprated to 7000 kW.

9801	**EB**	ET	CO		LESLEY GARRETT
9802	**EB**	ET	CO		STUART BURROWS
9803	**EB**	ET	CO		BENJAMIN LUXON
9804	**EB**	ET	CO		VICTORIA DE LOS ANGELES
9806	**EB**	ET	CO		REGINE CRESPIN
9808	**EB**	ET	CO		ELISABETH SODERSTROM
9809	**EB**	ET	CO		
9810	**EB**	ET	CO		JEAN-PHILIPPE COURTIS
9812	**EB**	ET	CO		LUCIANO PAVAROTTI
9814	**EB**	ET	CO		LUCIA POPP
9816	**EB**	ET	CO		WILLARD WHITE
9817	**EB**	ET	CO	(S)	JOSÉ CARRERAS
9819	**EB**	ET	CO		MARIA EWING
9820	**EB**	ET	CO		NICOLAI GHIAROV
9821	**EB**	ET	CO		TERESA BERGANZA
9823	**EB**	ET	CO		DAME ELISABETH LEGGE-SCHWARZKOPF
9825	**EB**	ET	CO		
9827	**EB**	ET	CO		BARBARA HENDRICKS
9828	**EB**	ET	CO		DAME KIRI TE KANAWA
9831	**EB**	ET	CO		
9832	**EB**	ET	CO		RENATA TEBALDI
9834	**EB**	ET	CO		MIRELLA FRENI
9835	**EB**	ET	CO		NICOLAI GEDDA
9838	**EB**	ET	CO		HILDEGARD BEHRENS
9840	**EB**	ET	CO		

4. LOCOMOTIVES AWAITING DISPOSAL

Locomotives that are still extant but best classed as awaiting disposal are listed here.

Class 58

| 58012 | Battlefield Line |
| 58023 | Battlefield Line |

Class 66

| 66048 | EMD, Longport Works |

5. LOCOMOTIVES EXPORTED FOR USE ABROAD

This section details former British Railways (plus privatisation era) diesel and electric locomotives that have been exported from the UK for use in industrial locations or with a main line operator abroad. Not included are locos that are "preserved" abroad, which are included in the Platform 5 "Preserved Locomotives of British Railways" publication. (S) denotes locomotives that are stored.

Number Other no./name   Location

Class 03

03156		Ferramenta Pugliese, Terlizzi, Bari, Italy

Class 47

47375	92 70 00 47375-5	Continental Railway Solution, Hungary

Class 56

56101	92 55 0659 001-5	FLOYD, Hungary
56115	92 55 0659 002-3	FLOYD, Hungary
56117	92 55 0659 003-1	FLOYD, Hungary (S) Budapest Keleti

Class 58

58001		DB, France, (S) Alizay
58004		DB, France, (S) Alizay
58005		DB, France, (S) Alizay
58006		DB, France, (S) Alizay
58007		DB, France, (S) Alizay
58009		DB, France, (S) Alizay
58010		DB, France, (S) Alizay
58011		DB, France, (S) Alizay
58013		DB, France, (S) Alizay
58015	L54	Transfesa, Spain, Monforte del Cid, Alicante
58018		DB, France, (S) Alizay
58020	L43	Transfesa, Spain, Monforte del Cid, Alicante
58021		DB, France, (S) Alizay
58024	L42	Transfesa, Spain, Monforte del Cid, Alicante
58025		DB, Spain, (S) Albacete
58026		DB, France, (S) Alizay
58027	L52	DB, Spain, (S) Albacete
58029	L44	Transfesa, Spain, (S) Monforte del Cid, Alicante
58030	L46	Transfesa, Spain, Monforte del Cid, Alicante
58031	L45	Transfesa, Spain, Monforte del Cid, Alicante
58032		DB, France, (S) Alizay
58033		DB, France, (S) Alizay
58034		DB, France, (S) Alizay
58035		DB, France, (S) Alizay
58036		DB, France, (S) Alizay
58038		DB, France, (S) Alizay

58039		DB, France, (S) Alizay
58040		DB, France, (S) Alizay
58041	L36	Transfesa, Spain, (S) Albacete
58042		DB, France, (S) Alizay
58043	L37	Transfesa, Spain, Monforte del Cid, Alicante
58044		DB, France, (S) Woippy, Metz
58046		DB, France, (S) Alizay
58047	L51	Transfesa, Spain, Monforte del Cid, Alicante
58049		DB, France, (S) Alizay
58050	L53	DB, Spain, (S) Albacete

Class 66

66010	ECR, France	66195	ECR, France	66235		ECR, France
66022	ECR, France	66196	DBC, Poland	66236		ECR, France
66026	ECR, France	66201	ECR, France	66237		DBC, Poland
66028	ECR, France	66202	ECR, France	66239		ECR, France
66029	ECR, France	66203	ECR, France	66240		ECR, France
66032	ECR, France	66204	ECR, France	66241		ECR, France
66033	ECR, France	66205	ECR, France	66242		ECR, France
66036	ECR, France	66208	ECR, France	66243		ECR, France
66038	ECR, France	66209	ECR, France	66244		ECR, France
66042	ECR, France	66210	ECR, France	66245		ECR, France
66045	ECR, France	66211	ECR, France	66246		ECR, France
66049	ECR, France	66212	ECR, France	66247		ECR, France
66052	ECR, France	66213	ECR, France	66248		DBC, Poland
66062	ECR, France	66214	ECR, France	66249		ECR, France
66064	ECR, France	66215	ECR, France	66411	66013	FL, Poland
66071	ECR, France	66216	ECR, France	66412	66015	FL, Poland
66072	ECR, France	66217	ECR, France	66417	66014	FL, Poland
66073	ECR, France	66218	ECR, France	66527	66016	FL, Poland
66123	ECR, France	66219	ECR, France	66530	66017	FL, Poland
66146	DBC, Poland	66220	DBC, Poland	66535	66018	FL, Poland
66153	DBC, Poland	66222	ECR, France	66582	66009	FL, Poland
66157	DBC, Poland	66223	ECR, France	66583	66010	FL, Poland
66159	DBC, Poland	66224	ECR, France	66584	66011	FL, Poland
66163	DBC, Poland	66225	ECR, France	66586	66008	FL, Poland
66166	DBC, Poland	66226	ECR, France	66595		FL, Poland
66173	DBC, Poland	66227	DBC, Poland	66608	66603	FL, Poland
66178	DBC, Poland	66228	ECR, France	66609	66605	FL, Poland
66179	ECR, France	66229	ECR, France	66611	66604	FL, Poland
66180	DBC, Poland	66231	ECR, France	66612	66606	FL, Poland
66189	DBC, Poland	66232	ECR, France	66624	66602	FL, Poland
66190	ECR, France	66233	ECR, France	66625	66601	FL, Poland
66191	ECR, France	66234	ECR, France	66954		FL, Poland
66193	ECR, France					

Class 86

86213	91 52 00 87703-2 Lancashire Witch	Bulmarket, Bulgaria
86215	91 55 0450 005-8	FLOYD, Hungary
86217	91 55 0450 006-6	FLOYD, Hungary
86218	91 55 0450 004-1	FLOYD, Hungary

86228	91 55 0450 007-4		FLOYD, Hungary
86231	91 52 00 85005-4	Lady of the Lake	Bulmarket, Bulgaria
86232	91 55 0450 003-3		FLOYD, Hungary
86233			Bulmarket, Bulgaria (S) Ruse
86234			Bulmarket, Bulgaria
86235	91 52 00 87704-0	Novelty	Bulmarket, Bulgaria
86242	91 55 0450 008-2		FLOYD, Hungary
86248	91 55 0450 001-7		FLOYD, Hungary
86250	91 55 0450 002-5		FLOYD, Hungary
86424	91 55 0450 009-0		FLOYD, Hungary (S) Budapest
86701	91 52 00 87701-6	Orion	Bulmarket, Bulgaria
86702	91 52 00 87702-4	Cassiopeia	Bulmarket, Bulgaria

Class 87

87003	91 52 00 87003-7		BZK, Bulgaria
87004	91 52 00 87004-5	Britannia	BZK, Bulgaria
87006	91 52 00 87006-0		BZK, Bulgaria
87007	91 52 00 87007-8		BZK, Bulgaria
87008	87008-9		BZK, Bulgaria (S) Ruse
87009	91 52 00 87009-4		Bulmarket, Bulgaria
87010	91 52 00 87010-2		BZK, Bulgaria
87012	91 52 00 87012-8		BZK, Bulgaria
87013	91 52 00 87013-6		BZK, Bulgaria
87014	87014-7		BZK, Bulgaria (S) Sofia
87017	91 52 00 87017-7	Iron Duke	Bulmarket, Bulgaria
87019	91 52 00 87019-3		BZK, Bulgaria
87020	91 52 00 87020-1		BZK, Bulgaria
87022	91 52 00 87022-7		BZK, Bulgaria
87023	91 52 00 87023-5	Velocity	Bulmarket, Bulgaria
87025	91 52 00 87025-0		Bulmarket, Bulgaria
87026	91 52 00 87026-8		BZK, Bulgaria
87028	91 52 00 87028-4		BZK, Bulgaria
87029	91 52 00 87029-2		BZK, Bulgaria
87033	91 52 00 87033-4		BZK, Bulgaria
87034	91 52 00 87034-2		BZK, Bulgaria

Class 92

92001	91 53 0 472 002-1	Mircea Eliade	Transagent Rail, Croatia
92002	91 53 0 472 003-9	Lucian Blaga	Transagent Rail, Croatia
92003		Beethoven	DB Cargo, Romania (S)
92005	91 53 0 472-005-4		Transagent Rail, Croatia
92012	91 53 0 472 001-3	Mihai Eminescu	Transagent Rail, Croatia
92022		Charles Dickens	DB Cargo, Bulgaria (S) Aurubis
92024	91 53 0 472 004-7	Marin Preda	Transagent Rail, Croatia
92025	91 52 1 688 025-1	Oscar Wilde	DB Cargo, Bulgaria
92026		Britten	DB Cargo, Romania
92027	91 52 1 688 027-7	George Eliot	DB Cargo, Bulgaria
92030	91 52 1 688 030-1	Ashford	DB Cargo, Bulgaria
92034	91 52 1 688 034-3	Kipling	DB Cargo, Bulgaria
92039	91 53 0 472 006-2	Eugen Ionescu	DB Cargo, Romania

6. CODES

6.1. LIVERY CODES

Livery codes are used to denote the various liveries carried. It is impossible to list every livery variation which currently exists. In particular items ignored for this publication include minor colour variations, omission of logos and all numbering, lettering and brandings. Descriptions quoted are thus a general guide only. Logos as appropriate for each livery are normally deemed to be carried. The colour of the lower half of the bodyside is stated first.

AB	Arriva Trains Wales/Welsh Government sponsored dark blue.
AI	Aggregate Industries (green, light grey & blue).
AL	Advertising/promotional livery (see class heading for details).
AR	Anglia Railways (turquoise blue with a white stripe).
AW	Arriva Trains Wales/Welsh Government sponsored dark & light blue.
AZ	Advenza Freight (deep blue with green Advenza brandings).
B	BR blue.
BL	BR Revised blue with yellow cabs, grey roof, large numbers & logo.
CA	Caledonian Sleeper (dark blue).
CD	Cotswold Rail (silver with blue & red logo).
CE	BR Civil Engineers (yellow & grey with black cab doors & window surrounds).
CM	Chiltern Mainline loco-hauled (two-tone grey & silver with blue stripes).
CS	Colas Rail (yellow, orange & black).
CU	Corus (silver with red logos).
DB	DB Cargo (Deutsche Bahn red with grey roof and solebar).
DC	Devon & Cornwall Railways (metallic silver).
DG	BR Departmental (dark grey with black cab doors & window surrounds).
DI	New DRS {Class 68 style} (deep blue & aquamarine with compass logo).
DR	Direct Rail Services (dark blue with light blue or dark grey roof).
DS	Revised Direct Rail Services (dark blue, light blue & green. "Compass" logo).
E	English Welsh & Scottish Railway (maroon bodyside & roof with a broad gold bodyside band).
EA	East Midlands Trains revised HST (dark blue, orange & red).
EB	Eurotunnel (two-tone grey with a broad blue stripe).
EG	"EWS grey" (as **F** but with large yellow & red EWS logo).
EP	European Passenger Services (two-tone grey with dark blue roof).
EX	Europhoenix (silver, blue & red).
F	BR Trainload Freight (two-tone grey with black cab doors & window surrounds. Various logos).
FA	Fastline Freight (grey & black with white & orange stripes).
FB	First Group dark blue.
FE	Railfreight Distribution International (two tone-grey with black cab doors & dark blue roof).
FER	Fertis (light grey with a dark grey roof & solebar).
FF	Freightliner grey (two-tone grey with black cab doors & window surrounds. Freightliner logo).
FG	New Freightliner; Genesee & Wyoming style (orange with black & yellow lower bodyside stripes).

FH	Revised Freightliner {PowerHaul} (dark green with yellow ends & a grey stripe/buffer beam).
FL	Freightliner (dark green with yellow cabs).
FO	BR Railfreight (grey bodysides, yellow cabs & red lower bodyside stripe, large BR logo).
FR	Fragonset Railways (black with silver roof & a red bodyside band lined out in white).
FS	First Group (indigo blue with pink & white stripes).
G	BR Green (plain green, with white stripe on main line locomotives).
GA	Greater Anglia (white with a black stripe).
GB	GB Railfreight (blue with orange cantrail & solebar stripes, orange cabs).
GG	BR green (two-tone green).
GL	First Great Western locomotives (green with a gold stripe).
GW	Great Western Railway (TOC) dark green.
GY	Eurotunnel (grey & yellow).
HA	Hanson Quarry Products (dark blue/silver with oxide red roof).
HN	Harry Needle Railroad Company (orange with a black roof and solebar).
IC	BR InterCity (dark grey/white/red/white).
K	Black.
KB	Knorr-Bremse Rail UK (blue, white & light green).
LH	BR Loadhaul (black with orange cabsides).
LM	London Midland (white/grey & green with broad black stripe around the windows).
LW	LNWR (grey with a red solebar).
M	Maroon.
ML	BR Mainline Freight (aircraft blue with a silver stripe).
N	BR Network SouthEast (white & blue with red lower bodyside stripe, grey solebar & cab ends).
O	Non-standard (see class heading for details).
PC	Pullman Car Company (umber & cream with gold lettering lined out in gold).
RB	Riviera Trains Oxford blue.
RL	RMS Locotec (dark blue with light grey cabsides).
RO	Rail Operations Group (dark blue).
RS	Railway Support Services (grey with a red solebar).
RX	Rail Express Systems (dark grey & red with or without blue markings).
RZ	Royal Train revised (plain claret, no lining).
SD	Stagecoach/South West Trains outer suburban {Class 450 style} (deep blue, orange & red).
SL	Silverlink (indigo blue with white stripe, green lower body & yellow doors).
SI	ScotRail InterCity (light grey & grey with INTER7CITY branding).
SN	Southern (white & dark green with light green semi-circles at one end of each vehicle. Light grey band at solebar level).
SR	ScotRail – Scotland's Railways (dark blue with Scottish Saltire flag & white/light blue flashes).
ST	Stagecoach (blue with red cabs).
TP	TransPennine Express (silver, grey, blue & purple).
TT	Transmart Trains (all over green).
V	Virgin Trains (red with black doors extending into bodysides, three white lower bodyside stripes).
VE	Virgin Trains East Coast (red & white with black window surrounds).
VN	Belmond Northern Belle (crimson lake & cream lined out in gold).

VP Virgin Trains shunters (black with a large black & white chequered flag on the bodyside).
WA Wabtec Rail (black).
WC West Coast Railway Company maroon.
XC CrossCountry (two-tone silver with deep crimson ends and pink doors).
Y   Network Rail yellow.

6.2. OWNER CODES

The following codes are used to define the ownership details of the locomotives or rolling stock listed in this book. Codes shown indicate either the legal owner or "responsible custodian" of each vehicle.

20	Class 20189
37	Scottish Thirty-Seven Group
40	Class 40 Preservation Society
47	Stratford 47 Group
50	Class 50 Alliance
56	Class 56 Locomotives
70	7029 Clun Castle
71	71A Locomotives
90	37906 Group
2L	Class Twenty Locomotives
A	Angel Trains
AD	AV Dawson
AF	Arlington Fleet Services
AI	Aggregate Industries
AM	Alstom
AV	Arriva UK Trains
BD	Bardon Aggregates
BN	Beacon Rail
BT	Bombardier Transportation
CS	Colas Rail
DB	DB Cargo (UK)
DC	DC Rail
DP	Deltic Preservation Society
DR	Direct Rail Services
DT	The Diesel Traction Group
E	Eversholt Rail (UK)
EL	Electric Traction Limited
EM	East Midlands Trains
EP	Europhoenix
ER	European Metal Recycling
ET	Eurotunnel
EU	Eurostar International
FG	First Group
FL	Freightliner
GB	GB Railfreight
GW	Great Western Railway (assets of the Greater Western franchise)
HA	Hanson UK
HN	Harry Needle Railroad Company

HT	Hanson Traction
HU	Hunslet Engine Company
KB	Knorr-Bremse Rail UK
LD	Locomotive Diesels
LF	Lombard Finance
LO	Loram (UK)
LN	London Overground
MQ	Macquarie Group
MR	Mendip Rail
MW	Martin Walker
NB	Boden Rail Engineering
NM	National Museum of Science & Industry
NR	Network Rail
NS	Nemesis Rail
NY	North Yorkshire Moors Railway Enterprises
P	Porterbrook Leasing Company
PP	Peter Pan Locomotive Company
RL	Rail Management Services (trading as RMS Locotec)
RO	Rail Operations Group
RS	Railway Support Services
RU	Russell Logistics
SP	The Scottish Railway Preservation Society
ST	Shaun Wright
SU	SembCorp Utilities UK
TT	Transmart Trains
UR	UK Rail Leasing
VG	Victoria Group
WA	Wabtec Rail Group
WC	West Coast Railway Company
WM	West Midlands Trains

6.3. LOCOMOTIVE POOL CODES

Locomotives are split into operational groups ("pools") for diagramming and maintenance purposes. The codes used to denote these pools are shown in this publication.

AWCA	West Coast Railway Company operational locomotives.
AWCX	West Coast Railway Company stored locomotives.
CFOL	Class 50 Operations locomotives.
CFSL	Class 40 Preservation Society Locomotives.
COFS	Colas Rail Class 56.
COLO	Colas Rail Classes 66 & 70.
COLS	Colas Rail stored locomotives.
COTS	Colas Rail Classes 37 & 67.
DFGI	Freightliner Class 70.
DFHH	Freightliner Class 66/6.
DFJH	Freightliner Class 66/5. Fitted with tripcocks.
DFIM	Freightliner Class 66/5.
DFIN	Freightliner low emission Class 66.
DFLC	Freightliner Class 90.
DFNC	Freightliner Class 86/6.

DHLT	Freightliner locomotives awaiting maintenance/repair/disposal.
EFOO	Great Western Railway Class 57.
EFPC	Great Western Railway 43.
EHPC	CrossCountry Class 43.
EMPC	East Midlands Trains Class 43.
EPEX	Europhoenix locomotives for export.
EPUK	Europhoenix UK locomotives.
GBBR	GB Railfreight Class 73 for possible rebuilding.
GBBT	GB Railfreight Class 66. Large fuel tanks.
GBCH	GB Railfreight Class 86 & 87.
GBCS	GB Railfreight Class 73/9. Caledonian Sleeper.
GBDF	GB Railfreight Class 47.
GBEB	GB Railfreight Class 66. Ex-European, large fuel tanks.
GBED	GB Railfreight Class 73.
GBEE	GB Railfreight Class 20. On hire from HNRC.
GBEL	GB Railfreight Class 66. New build, small fuel tanks.
GBET	GB Railfreight Class 92. Stored locomotives.
GBFM	GB Railfreight Class 66. RETB fitted.
GBGS	GB Railfreight Class 56. Stored locomotives.
GBLT	GB Railfreight Class 66. Small fuel tanks.
GBNB	GB Railfreight Class 66. New build.
GBNR	GB Railfreight Class 73/9. Network Rail contracts.
GBOB	GB Railfreight Class 66. Former DB Cargo locomotives; large fuel tanks and buckeye couplers.
GBSL	GB Railfreight Class 92. Caledonian Sleeper.
GBST	GB Railfreight Class 92. Caledonian Sleeper & Channel Tunnel.
GBTG	GB Railfreight Class 60.
GBYH	GB Railfreight Class 59.
GROG	Rail Operations Group operational locomotives.
HAPC	ScotRail Class 43.
HNRL	Harry Needle Railroad Company hire locomotives.
HNRS	Harry Needle Railroad Company stored locomotives.
HTLX	Hanson Traction locomotives.
HYWD	South Western Railway Class 73.
IANA	Greater Anglia Class 90.
IECA	London North Eastern Railway Class 91.
IECP	London North Eastern Railway Class 43.
MBDL	Non TOC-owned diesel locomotives.
MBED	Non TOC-owned electro-diesel locomotives.
MBEL	Non TOC-owned electric locomotives.
MOLO	Class 20189 Ltd Class 20.
NRLO	Nemesis Rail locomotives.
QADD	Network Rail locomotives.
QCAR	Network Rail New Measurement Train Class 43.
QETS	Network Rail Class 37.
RVLO	Loram (UK) locomotives.
SROG	Rail Operations Group locomotives under overhaul.
UKRL	UK Rail Leasing. Operational locomotives.
UKRM	UK Rail Leasing. Locomotives for overhaul.
UKRS	UK Rail Leasing. Stored locomotives.
WAAC	DB Cargo Class 67.

WABC	DB Cargo Class 67. RETB fitted.
WACC	DB Cargo Class 67.
WAWC	DB Cargo Class 67 for hire to Transport for Wales.
WBAE	DB Cargo Class 66. Locomotives fitted with "stop-start" technology.
WBAR	DB Cargo Class 66. Fitted with remote monitoring equipment.
WBAT	DB Cargo Class 66.
WBBE	DB Cargo Class 66. RETB fitted and fitted with "stop-start" technology.
WBBT	DB Cargo Class 66. RETB fitted.
WBLE	DB Cargo Class 66. Dedicated locomotives for Lickey Incline banking duties. Fitted with "stop-start" technology.
WBLT	DB Cargo Class 66. Dedicated locomotives for Lickey Incline banking duties.
WBRT	DB Cargo Class 66. Railhead Treatment Train duties.
WCAT	DB Cargo Class 60.
WCBT	DB Cargo Class 60. Extended-range fuel tanks.
WDAM	DB Cargo Class 59.
WEAC	DB Cargo Class 90.
WEDC	DB Cargo Class 90 for hire to London North Eastern Railway.
WFBC	DB Cargo Class 92 with TVM430 cab signalling equipment for use on High Speed 1.
WQAA	DB Cargo stored locomotives Group 1A (short-term maintenance).
WQAB	DB Cargo stored locomotives Group 1B.
WQBA	DB Cargo stored locomotives Group 2 (unserviceable).
WQCA	DB Cargo stored locomotives Group 3 (unserviceable).
WQDA	DB Cargo stored locomotives Group 4 (awaiting disposal).
XHAC	Direct Rail Services Classes 37/4 & 57/3.
XHCC	Direct Rail Services Class 37/4. Cumbrian Coast passenger.
XHCE	Direct Rail Services Class 68 for hire to Chiltern Railways.
XHCK	Direct Rail Services Class 57/0.
XHIM	Direct Rail Services locomotives – Intermodal traffic.
XHNC	Direct Rail Services locomotives – nuclear traffic/general.
XHSS	Direct Rail Services stored locomotives.
XHTP	Direct Rail Services Class 68 for hire to TransPennine Express.
XHVE	Direct Rail Services Classes 68 & 88.
XHVT	Direct Rail Services Class 57/3 for hire to Virgin Trains.
XYPA	Mendip Rail Class 59/1.
XYPO	Mendip Rail Class 59/0.

6.4. ALLOCATION & LOCATION CODES

Allocation codes are used in this publication to denote the normal maintenance base ("depots") of each operational locomotive. However, maintenance may be carried out at other locations and also by mobile teams. The designation (S) denotes stored.

Code	Location	Depot Operator
BH	Barrow Hill (Chesterfield)	Barrow Hill Engine Shed Society
BM	Bournemouth	South Western Railway
BN	Bounds Green (London)	London North Eastern Railway
BO	Bo'ness (West Lothian)	The Bo'ness & Kinneil Railway
BQ	Bury (Greater Manchester)	East Lancashire Railway Trust
BU	Burton-upon-Trent	Nemesis Rail

CB	Crewe Basford Hall	Freightliner Engineering
CE	Crewe International	DB Cargo (UK)
CF	Cardiff Canton	Transport for Wales/Colas Rail
CL	Crewe LNWR Heritage	LNWR Heritage Company
CN	Castle Donington RFT	*Storage location only*
CO	Coquelles (France)	Eurotunnel
CR	Crewe Gresty Bridge	Direct Rail Services
CS	Carnforth	West Coast Railway Company
EC	Edinburgh Craigentinny	London North Eastern Railway
HO	Hope Cement Works	Hope Cement
HJ	Hoo Junction (Kent)	Colas Rail
HT	Heaton (Newcastle-upon-Tyne)	Northern/LNER
KM	Carlisle Kingmoor	Direct Rail Services
KR	Kidderminster	Severn Valley Railway
LA	Laira (Plymouth)	Great Western Railway
LB	Loughborough Works	Brush Traction
LD	Leeds Midland Road	Freightliner Engineering
LE	Landore (Swansea)	Great Western Railway
LM	Quinton Rail Technology Centre (Long Marston, Warwickshire)	Motorail Logistics
LR	Leicester	UK Rail Leasing
LT	Longport (Stoke-on-Trent)	ElectroMotive Diesel Services
LW	MoD Longtown (Cumbria)	*Storage location only*
MD	Merehead	Mendip Rail
NC	Norwich Crown Point	Greater Anglia
NL	Neville Hill (Leeds)	East Midlands Trains/Northern
NM	Nottingham Eastcroft	East Midlands Trains/Boden Rail
NY	Grosmont (North Yorkshire)	North Yorkshire Moors Railway Enterprises
RR	Doncaster Robert's Road	ElectroMotive Diesel Services
SC	Scunthorpe Steelworks	British Steel
SE	St Leonards (Hastings)	St Leonards Railway Engineering
SL	Stewarts Lane (London)	Govia Thameslink Railway/Belmond
SK	Swanwick West (Derbyshire)	The Princess Royal Locomotive Trust
SW	Swanage	Swanage Railway
TM	Tyseley Locomotive Works	Vintage Trains
TO	Toton (Nottinghamshire)	DB Cargo (UK)
WB	Wembley (London)	Alstom
WN	Willesden (London)	Bombardier Transportation
WO	Wolsingham, Weardale Railway	RMS Locotec
YK	National Railway Museum (York)	National Museum of Science & Industry
ZA	RTC Business Park (Derby)	Loram (UK)
ZB	Doncaster Works	Wabtec Rail
ZC	Crewe Works	Bombardier Transportation UK
ZD	Derby Works	Bombardier Transportation UK
ZG	Eastleigh Works	Arlington Fleet Services
ZH	Springburn Depot (Glasgow)	Knorr-Bremse Rail Systems (UK)
ZI	Ilford Works	Bombardier Transportation UK
ZJ	Stoke-on-Trent Works	Axiom Rail (Stoke)
ZK	Kilmarnock Caledonia Works	Wabtec Rail Scotland
ZM	Kilmarnock Bonnyton Works	Brodie Engineering
ZN	Wolverton Works	Knorr-Bremse Rail Systems (UK)
ZR	Holgate Works (York)	Network Rail